James Harkin is a social forecaster and director of *Flockwatching*. He writes regularly for the *Financial Times* and the *Guardian*, and is the author of *Cyburbia* and *Big Ideas*.

For more information, visit www.flockwatching.com and www.jamesharkin.co.uk

Also by James Harkin

Cyburbia

Niche

Why the Market No Longer Favours the Mainstream

JAMES HARKIN

Little, Brown

To Giulia Ricci

LITTLE, BROWN

First published in Great Britain in 2011 by Little, Brown

A CIP catalogue record for this book is available from the British Library.

Hardback ISBN 978-1-4087-0326-7
C-Format ISBN 978-1-4087-0243-7

Typeset in Garamond by M Rules
Printed and bound in Great Britain by
Clays Ltd, St Ives plc

Little, Brown
An imprint of
Little, Brown Book Group
100 Victoria Embankment
London EC4Y 0DY

An Hachette UK Company
www.hachette.co.uk

www.littlebrown.co.uk

Contents

Introduction

The Missing Middle and the Gap

It started with loud music. Sometime in the year 1999, staff at outlets of the clothing retailer Gap in New York and San Francisco became aware that one of their rivals on the shopping mall, Abercrombie & Fitch, was playing ear-splitting electronic dance music inside its stores. The strategy was deliberate. While Gap was ushering everyone into its stores – its fashions were ageless, its interiors sparsely decorated and its legions of cheery greeters would say hello to just about anyone – Abercrombie & Fitch had become openly hostile to anyone over thirty. Not only that, but it was doing its utmost to drive them away, which was why it was instructing its staff to play music loud enough that they wouldn't be able to hear themselves think. Abercrombie was also warding off unwanted customers by putting dark shades on its windows. If any oldies still hadn't got the message, it had some of its more modish teenage employees hover by the door.

Unfortunately for Gap's executives, it seemed to be working. Trend-obsessed youngsters were flooding out of department stores like Gap and into hipper retailers – Abercrombie & Fitch and J.Crew for preppy teenagers, American Apparel and H&M for hipsters in their twenties – which had carved themselves out a niche by zeroing in on the younger shopper. They received a warm welcome. For several years, New York's febrile trend-spotters had been telling anyone who would listen that the spending habits of Americans born between 1977 and 1994 – what they called Generation Y, or the Echo Boomers – were going to go through the roof. They had statistics to prove it. America's teenage population had been rising every year since 1992, and was forecast to continue to grow until 2010; even better, thanks to their indulgent parents their spending was growing at a phenomenal rate.

After carefully examining the figures, Gap's executives decided to go follow that and go trendy. To lure the capricious younger crowd back into its stores, it began to stock tiny little tops and bright pink trousers, hoodies and clingy sweaters, miniskirts and babydoll dresses. It hired the über-cool R&B singer Macy Gray to front its advertising campaign, began to produce a line of leather trousers and even flirted with playing music in some of its stores. The results were disastrous. Perhaps seeing through Gap's shameless about-turn, teenagers and young adults continued to ignore it in favour of places like Abercrombie & Fitch that were more single-minded about winning their custom. Worse still, Gap's once loyal over-35 customers were royally offended by the new approach and began their own exodus to stores that were cheaper, or quieter, or which simply stocked clothes they wanted to wear.

Gap's managers were nonplussed because, for as long as any of them could remember, population trends had been going their way. The first Gap store was opened in 1969 amid the ferment of California's counter-culture, and the name was inspired by the generation gap that had opened up between rebellious young hippies and their frumpy parents. With its unfussy, easy-to-wear jeans and casuals that could be worn by just about anyone, Gap made it its mission to bridge that generation gap. For a long time it succeeded, and the company's phenomenal growth in the following decades rode the wave of a casual look that everyone seemed to like. The store had something for everyone: young people went there to buy T-shirts, grandmothers went there to buy cardigans, everyone went there to buy khakis. In 1982 Gap set up its own label (before that it had sold mainly Levi's jeans) and in 1983 it bought the safari-themed clothes firm Banana Republic; in the years after it expanded into Europe and Asia, rolled out its children lines GapKids and babyGap, and launched Old Navy, a cheaper chain of stores. By the late nineties Gap had became the biggest clothing retailer in the world, with three thousand stores across its three main brands Gap, Banana Republic and Old Navy. It was worn by everyone from *Vogue* models to Sharon Stone, who, in 1996, delighted the company's executives by turning up on the red carpet at the Oscars wearing a charcoal-grey turtleneck that she told journalists was from Gap. It was around this time, too, that Gap became the byword for a shift towards office casual wear. It was as if it had become the official supplier of the new workplace uniform – one of chinos and plain T-shirts, that made everyone look the same as everyone else.

Then, all of a sudden, no one seemed to want to wear a uniform. Whereas just a few years before Gap had appealed to both teenagers and their parents, now it seemed that neither of them would be seen dead in any store frequented by the other. In the summer of 2002, Gap's executives realised that courting fickle young adults had driven away many of their previously loyal older customers and achieved nothing. 'We understand we've alienated teenagers,' its vice-president of marketing Kyle Andrew told *Women's Wear Daily*, 'but we want to go after people who knew us and loved us.' It was the closest the company came to an apology to its older customers, and it was accompanied by an advertising blitzkrieg aimed at wooing them back. Under the slogan 'For Every Generation: Gap', the company unveiled a dizzyingly cross-generational range of musicians and celebrities smiling and jigging around to upbeat music. Veteran country singer-songwriter Willie Nelson was drafted in to play alongside the youthful Ryan Adams; Gena Rowlands was paired up with Salma Hayek; Sissy Spacek with Natalie Imbruglia. None of it worked. Gap's store sales continued to plummet – by the end of 2002 they'd been falling away for twenty-nine months in a row, one of the worst performances in its history. 'It's hard to nail down the Gap's target customer,' sniffed one retail analyst. 'It's everybody, and if you're all things to everybody, you're nobody.' Gap had abandoned the broad middle market because it had become obsessed with losing its youth. But by the time it owned up to its mistake and tried to put the middle back together again, it discovered that it no longer existed.

2

This book is about what happened next. It's about a world in which no size fits all, and in which anyone who tries to be all things to everyone ends up as nothing to anyone. The missing middle has its origins in social changes going back many decades, but it has recently gathered pace to become the single most important social phenomenon of our times. The middle has withered at such different rates in different walks of life that many of us have failed to appreciate it. Its disappearance, however, has coloured much of what we do, from the way we identify ourselves to the things that we buy, from the television programmes we watch to the newspapers we read, from the messages we hear from our politicians to the way that we go about finding a partner. Out of it has emerged a strange new universe in which everyone wants to be different, and everything has its niche.

One way of thinking about this is to turn to ecology. Social scientists tend to see us humans as the top of the food chain, the big beasts around whom everything revolves. Ecologists, on the other hand, prefer to see us as just another species on a larger canvas – an all-encompassing web of ecosystems, thickly populated with different creatures none of which can be said to have overall control. One of the fathers of modern ecology was Charles Darwin. In *On the Origin of Species*, Darwin was one of the first to think about plant and animal life as populations. It was by examining variations in the characteristics of those populations over time that Darwin was able to arrive at his principle of natural selection, and the idea of the survival of the fittest.

To track those populations, ecologists need to know their niche. The niche of a species refers to its nesting places and how it fits into its surrounding ecosystem, which largely depends on what it eats and what eats it. Think of it as a combination of where it lives and what it does. In the last decade, we have all been thrown into what looks very like an ecosystem. It used to be that our consumption was tightly controlled by a few big corporate beasts. We were their captive audience; they knew who we were, our appetites seemed predictable enough and so they all fed us much the same thing. Now, however, they've emerged blinking into a new environment populated by many different species, each of which seems to want different things. Think about what happened to Gap. For several decades it bounded along like an eight-hundred-pound gorilla until, around the year 2000, it came up against a massive and unexpected crevasse. Gap stumbled around blindly in this new ecosystem, charging this way and that because it lacked a clear niche.

What has happened to the big beasts matters because they held the reins of mainstream culture. Mainstream is often used to mean stuff that is merely popular or which happens to prevail, but I want to argue that mainstream culture only emerged in the middle decades of the twentieth century, and under the supervision of a few big beasts. In its heyday, it was a shifting and dynamic force, powerful enough to sweep up almost anything into it. Most of all, it opened up a middle ground on which we could all walk. In the last few decades, however, it has broken down. The big beasts have never quite recovered. They're not quite big enough to control a whole ecosystem. On the other hand, they are not sufficiently lean or focused to know their place within it. Just like Gap, they have been left stuck in the middle, known by everyone but loved by no one. They have done their best to adapt to their new environment. Some of them have fought a desperate rearguard action, spreading themselves perilously thin in an effort to remain all things to all people. Others have hired hunter-gatherers, who have used an impressive army of weapons and traps to identify and target individual sections of the audience. The more audacious have even been looking underground, going after subcultures that have traditionally defined themselves against mainstream culture. So far, results have been mixed. What has become clear, though, is that slicing up one's customers into sections in order to go after each of them one at a time is an inexact science that does not often work as well as its practitioners claim. It also makes the middle ground look even less inviting.

3

I should also declare an interest. In 2000, just at the time Gap was beginning to struggle with the missing middle, I was a hired hand working for the big beasts. Not only that, I was one of those New York trend-spotters vigorously sending companies this way and that in search of a quick buck.

Like many others, I'd been drafted in to help big companies get to know their audiences better. My job title was futurologist, but that was a little grand. For the most part, all I was doing was carving up the audience in different ways in order to predict how it might behave in the near future. That the big beasts needed help from people like me is revealing. They just didn't know who their audience was any more. Like natural scientists, their response was to put it under the microscope and focus ever more intensely on its characteristics, identifying species and sub-species within it to work out what each of them might do next. In the absence of anything better, the characteristics they identified us by were our income, age, education, gender and race. And, just as naturalists venture out into the field in search of interesting specimens, they paid clipboard-carrying pollsters and market researchers to go out among populations, talking to small samples in order to find out what made everyone tick. By the year 2000 those attempts at field-work had become outlandish, which is whey they'd hired trend-spotters, cool-hunters and future-gazers like me. We were given lots of interesting data and intelligence to work with, and many of the predictions we arrived at were valuable attempts to track social change. In those heady days at the turn of the millennium, though, it's fair to say that we were making a lot of it up.

Looking back, I think we were aiming at the wrong targets. Maybe we were looking in the wrong places too. What we didn't know then was that online communication would bring entirely new threats to the big beasts. Snapping at their heels in this new environment are strange new beings who nibble away at their girth, or who can race past them on the way to their prey. The audience, too, has begun to change shape. The internet has made us more hawkish in seeking out exactly what we're after, and there's plenty to choose from.

The bigger the ecosystem, it turns out, the more likely it is that new species will proliferate and a diverse bounty of flora and fauna will thrive. And just as our environment is growing more diverse, so is our diet. Our new landscape is brimming with exotic minutiae of all different shapes and sizes, and we're bunching together in the places we find it. These new nesting places cater for our passion to be different much better than the big beasts ever did; many of them take great pride in defining themselves as apart from the mainstream, in a club of their own. One way or another, we're all huddling together now.

None of this can be held responsible for the crack-up of the mainstream. Mainstream culture was built upon solid foundations in society, economy and political life. In its heyday it spanned not only the stuff that we buy but the books that we read and the films and television that we watch. It helped bind us together for a while, but as its foundations have fallen away it has become bloated and slow, easy prey for the newer and more agile creatures who are moving on to its turf. Survival in this new terrain, however, is not of the fittest but of those with the best fit with their environment. More than anything, it depends on finding something you feel strongly about and cultivating it. Find a clear niche and you make it fantastically easy for people to find you. Fail to do so and you risk ending up on the list of endangered species.

1

Out of the Whale

The rise and fall of mainstream culture

On how the big beasts tried to scoop us all up and sank to the bottom

The year 2009 was one of mass extinctions, and no more so than on the British high street. One after another, long-time staples of British retailing filed for bankruptcy, their once thriving stores boarded up. By the middle of the year, reckoned one survey, 15 per cent of retail floorspace was empty, with some town centres recording a vacancy rate of two out of every five shops. Many looked like ghost towns. The biggest gap was left by the sudden departure of Woolworths. For as long as anyone could remember, Woolworths had been one of the most familiar names on the British high street. Amid plunging sales and debts of £385 million, however, it turned out the lights on the last of its eight hundred stores on 5 January, ending a century of trading.

In the months following Woolworths' demise, an extended public wake was played out in the local and national media. On internet bulletin boards, thousands of people took the trouble to write personal farewells. It wasn't hard to fathom why everyone was so fond of the place. Woolworths was once the everyman of high-street stores, the first place many British and Irish people had ever bought anything from. The Belfast city centre branch was where I had picked up my first record, in the early eighties. When I moved to London to study, it was to the local Woolworths that I went in search of my first set of cutlery. Woolworths was for everyone; if there was anything you wanted and couldn't find anywhere else, you could always be sure to find it at Woolies. There were jumpers, alarm clocks, skipping ropes and saucepans; shoe polish, curtains, mops and safety pins; paint-brushes, pillowcases, ironing boards and candles; thermos flasks, hair-straightening irons, hula hoops, bread bins and buckets and spades. It was all there, piled high in narrow aisles, and somehow it all seemed to make perfect sense. By the summer of 2009, some stores had been taken over by artists. One Sunday in early July I visited the Woolworths on Leytonstone High Road in East London, where fifty-five local artists had come together to pay their respects with personal reminders of working and shopping in the store. Visitors had followed suit, leaving Post-it notes on the store noticeboard. Here are some of them:

I really miss you, Woolies, have all those vital but unnecessary ingredients that I want in one place. It's like the death of a relation.

There's nowhere to buy zips and buttons, now that Woolies has closed down.

I stole a red purse from Woolies, when I was five.

Woolies RIP.

Ah, Woolies: where kids could be threatened with working, if they didn't study hard.

I'm really going to miss the pick 'n' mix. RIP Woolies.

The title of the show was Pick 'n' Mix, and it seemed utterly appropriate. Pick 'n' mix was the name for the selection of chocolates and boiled sweets that became Woolworths' most famous product line. When I was growing up the sweets were laid out in a circular rack of tubs, and patrons were invited to scoop into a paper bag what they wanted – cola cubes, pear drops, midget gems, white chocolate mice, strawberry bonbons, chocolate raisins, jelly beans and wrapped sweets. We youngsters would stand around, helping ourselves to the occasional free sample. Woolies was like that: an eclectic free-for-all open to absolutely everyone.

In the outbreak of public nostalgia, however, there were a few nagging anomalies. The store was finally killed off by fall-out from the global economic downturn, but everyone knew that its problems went back much further. Despite all their fondness for the store, no one I met at that art show in East London had actually shopped there for years.

Then there was the question of its nationality. To hear people memorialise it, anyone would be forgiven for thinking that Woolies was a part of the national heritage, as British as roast beef. In fact, it was as American as apple pie. On 22 February 1879, a moustachioed, cigar-loving American farmer's son called Frank Winfield Woolworth opened the doors of the first F. W. Woolworth outlet in Utica, in his home state of New York.

The idea of selling all kinds of general merchandise dated back to the covered markets of medieval Europe, but it had long fallen out of favour. By the middle of the nineteenth century, retail districts in town and city centres were home to a variety of small traders, each of whom – the draper, the grocer, the hatter, the shoemaker – had become specialists in selling their own wares. Frank Woolworth, however, decided that the general store was due for a comeback, and in a new kind of way. Whereas most tradesmen had allowed their customers to haggle, Woolworth decided to charge the same low fixed price for everything – five cents – and treat all his customers in exactly the same way. Shopkeepers had tended to keep their merchandise out of reach of their customers behind a counter, but Frank Woolworth had the idea of laying out his wares in long aisles on the shop floor, so that anyone could see and touch it prior to purchase. The result looked very much like a pick 'n' mix of stuff, a selection whose only common denominator was that it had all been selected by Woolworth himself. His first, New York store was a failure – it was too far away from a town centre – but his second attempt, in Lancaster, Pennsylvania a month later, proved an immediate success, possibly because by then Woolworth had thought to vary his range to two fixed prices, five and ten cents. Thus was born 'five and dime' retailing, and the modern variety store.

Much of the success of Woolworth's five and dime stores was due to his ability to buy in huge quantities directly from manufacturers, thereby reducing costs and cutting out the middle-men. The plan was to get people into the store and then, by constantly expanding the variety of goods on offer, to build a captive audience. To help propel passers-by into his stores, Woolworth hired orchestras and singing groups to perform outside, and pipe-organists to patrol the aisles. Soon they would have little choice in the matter. Since there was only room for one big general store in many streets and small towns, Woolworth realised that if he moved fast he could secure a monopoly. He seems to have taken much the same approach to his personal life. Woolworth the rambunctious bon vivant was known for his imposing stomach, and kept an impressive array of rich foods available all day and night – everything from lobsters to bananas – in his apartment just in case he should feel the urge for a snack. During a visit to Paris, he is said to have rented a whole floor of a Parisian hotel and a selection of the city's prostitutes.

Frank Woolworth's pick 'n' mix approach to general retailing and his idea of the variety store was not popular with everyone. The local shopkeepers he drove out of business were incensed at his arrogance. His retail strategy, however, proved an enormous success and his idea of the variety store would go on to change the way people shopped. Woolworth's prices were cheap, but his approach was far from tawdry. His aim, according to one journalist, was to offer 'highbrow retail at lowbrow prices'. He branded his stationery with the upwardly mobile Fifth Avenue label, and called his perfume Evening in Paris. By 1900 he was in possession of fifty-four stores in major cities of the United States, and soon after that he began to look abroad. 'I believe,' Woolworth wrote in his diary during one of his regular visits to Britain, 'that a good penny and sixpence store, run by a live Yankee, would be a sensation here.'

The first British outlet was opened in Liverpool in 1909, with fixed prices of threepence and sixpence. It was between the thirties and the fifties, however, that the store really began to thrive, and it was then that many of its most strikingly art deco stores were built. By the early thirties Woolworth was opening a new UK store every seventeen days and, such was his purchasing power, that the numbers involved were often mind-boggling. By 1930, Woolworth's American stores were selling four thousand miles of pencils every year; twenty years later, they were shifting 250 million pounds' worth of chewing gum. The store continued to expand aggressively through the sixties and seventies, often buying competitor stores, and by 1979 F. W. Woolworth had become the biggest department store in the world. Soon after that, however, its fortunes began to turn sour. In the eighties, its once loyal customers began to drift away to shopping malls or superstores – such as Wal-Mart and CostCo in the United States, or Tesco and Asda in the UK – which had sprung up out on the outskirts of towns and cities. Woolworths' selection began to look tired and limited. When those superstores moved beyond their core business of selling food to stock just about everything else, its fate was sealed. On a visit to Wal-Mart, shoppers could buy all the food they needed and then amble around in an enormous space where they could be sure to find anything else that they wanted too. Or they could it pick up on the net, from vast virtual supermarkets that seem to stock just about everything. Those that still did shop on the high street preferred a new species of sharply discounted stores with names like Poundland or Dollar General, which borrowed Woolworth's idea of selling everything at the same fixed price. Woolworths was no longer able to generate what retail analysts call footfall – enough feet walking through the door to justify its purchasing power and its reputation as a general retailer. In many ways, its collapse in the UK was long overdue. In 1982 its American parent had sold off Woolworths' British stores to a retail consortium, and in 1994 it had parted with its Canadian operation too. The last Woolworths store in the United States shut its doors in 1997. In the same year the company was replaced in the Dow Jones stock market index by Wal-Mart.

In the post-mortem that followed Woolworths' demise in the UK, the immediate cause of death was not difficult to establish. Woolies was a high-street general store in a world that no longer had much need for high-street general stores. While Woolworths had stood still, supermarkets, shopping malls and online retailers had grown big enough to gather every kind of brand and product on to their turf, becoming self-contained universes. Woolworths wasn't big enough to compete, nor was it focused enough to offer a tightly defined range of products at cheaper than cheap prices. It was stuck in the middle and it got run over.

Woolworths' products were not necessarily shoddy, but the reason why they had been lumped together in one place and how they had been priced were no longer clear. Its executives tried hard to get their stores to sell more of what they were good at – entertainment, toys, homewares, children's clothes and pick 'n' mix – but they also took steps to standardise the stock at each of their store. Claire Robertson, a plain-speaking woman in her mid-thirties who started out doing Saturday shifts at Woolies and worked her worked her way up to become manager of its Dorchester branch, remembers being frustrated by the strategy of her bosses. 'What they tried to be was identical in every single store,' she says, 'to be a little bit of everything.' The result, she felt, was to leave her little room to focus on what her store was good at selling, which was children's toys, clothes and books. In the face of rising rents, Woolies stores also devoted more space to popular entertainment products, to what Robertson describes as 'middle-of-the-road DVDs and CDs, which people could find anywhere else'. This was a shame, because if Woolworths' pick 'n' mix approach to general retailing wasn't working, a few of its specialist areas were still doing surprisingly well. Until it collapsed, Woolworths' former chief executive Trevor Bish-Jones reminded me, Woolies was still the third biggest retailer of children's clothes in the UK. The pick 'n' mix counter was holding up well too, but since Woolies closed that side of the business had been snapped up by sweet shops and cinema foyers, where prices tended to be higher. 'And I know for a fact,' he said, his voice narrowing to a conspiratorial whisper, 'that the quality of the product is rubbish.'

Woolworths wouldn't be the first big beast to come up against its own mortality in the course of 2009. In Britain it would soon be followed by the entertainment retailer Zavvi, which began closing its stores at the end of January. In America General Motors, one of the biggest beasts of all, would take refuge in bankruptcy in June of that year, and in July it was joined by that giant of general-interest magazines, *Reader's Digest*. Woolworths, however, was the first to go that year. It had staked out its terrain on the British high street for a hundred years, and specialised in serving a pre-digested pick 'n' mix of things that it thought were good for us. It was as if it and other big beasts like it had held us captive in their bellies, the better to feed us more stuff. For a long time we were glad of what they gave us, but eventually we began to make for the exit. In their desperation to scoop us all up, many big beasts stretched themselves so thin that they ended up satisfying no one. They surrendered any authority they had over the products that they sold and ended up looking generic.

But just how did we end up so captive to them in the first place, and how did we manage to escape? It is important that we know the answer, because the rise and fall of stores like Woolworths is also a story about the rise and fall of the general public.

2

In the early eighties, on the days when I wasn't hovering around the pick 'n' mix counter at Woolworths I was in front of the TV. The first film I have any memory of watching was *Gone with the Wind*, the story of a headstrong Georgia girl and her journey to womanhood amid the horrors of the American Civil War. *Gone with the Wind* was a family film, and I remember us all being there; my father ostensibly asleep but with one eye open, my sister and I hunkered dutifully around the television, my mother gleefully stealing all the best lines – 'Frankly, my dear, I don't give a damn' and 'Great balls of fire' – by hollering them out in advance. On its release in 1939, the film was Hollywood at its most ambitious and its most extravagant: the most expensive film ever made and, at nearly four hours long, one of the longest. It didn't matter, because it would also turn out to be the most popular film ever made. In its first cinematic release, at a time when America's population was only 130 million, *Gone with the Wind* broke all box office records, selling 202 million tickets. In a vintage year for cinema, it competed with *The Wizard of Oz*, *Of Mice and Men* and *Stagecoach* at the Academy Awards and swept the board to win a then-record eight Oscars, including Best Picture.

Gone with the Wind was made to be watched on the big screen, and it is difficult for us to imagine the excitement that must have accompanied its first cinematic run. Back then there were no DVDs or internet downloads. Films were like a visiting circus: miss them when they were in town and chances were they would not come around again for years. Even now, in the dark, holding us quietly hypnotised by its huge beam of light, cinema is still the most impressive example of how a mass medium can hold an audience captive in their seats. It is difficult to underestimate the power that Hollywood's big beasts had over us as we sat in the cinema in the years before television arrived in our living rooms. *Gone with the Wind* was a triumph for the legendary producer David O. Selznick, a meddlesome perfectionist with a stubborn, implacable vision who did more than anyone else to see the film through. It was Selznick who staked his career and most of his fortune on it, holding his nerve as the costs began to spiral out of control.

The release of *Gone with the Wind* also marked the coming of age of the studio system, in which the big five Hollywood studios – MGM, the studio that invested in Selznick's film, Paramount, Warner, Twentieth Century Fox and RKO – controlled the whole movie-making business from beginning to end. Not only did they churn out films, but many of them also distributed those films and came to own the cinemas that played them too. It was a mammoth undertaking. Creating *Gone with the Wind*, for example, was an industrial production every bit as complicated as a factory assembly line. One report, from the set, from the *Macon Telegraph* on 19 March 1939, was breathless in its admiration for a world in which 'cameras are no longer cranked by hand. Electricity does the work. There is enough electric current used on the stages at Selznick International Pictures in one day to provide lights for a small city.' *Gone with the Wind* was made with a cast of thousands of extras, and shot with a film technology – the garishly beautiful Technicolor – which was then only four years young. Its epic portrayal of a burning, war-torn Atlanta, for example, was mostly mounted and shot even before Vivien Leigh had been hired, and all twelve of the available Technicolor cameras in Hollywood were marshalled for the shoot.

The film's phenomenal success was about more than machinery. Techniques for mass production were not at all new in 1939: in fact, they had been around since the early nineteenth century, when ordinary workers were uprooted from the countryside to work long hours in city factories. Those workers needed to be fed and clothed, and so production lines sprang up to do that too. The feat of producing identical goods aimed at large numbers of people meant that factory owners had to identify sizeable common denominators in the market. By the 1860s, for example, a third of all employees of the American garment industry were knocking out hoop skirts, which means large numbers of American women must have found themselves wearing the same thing.

It wasn't long before those uprooted country workers began to crave a little entertainment. Cinema, a new kind of industrially produced culture designed for consumption by large numbers of people, was just the ticket. Its first commercial outing came at a Paris café in 1895, when the Lumière brothers charged an admission fee for a forty-five-second film of workers leaving the Lumière factory in Lyon. Here was the audience for the new mass medium reflected back to themselves, but it took another four decades for that audience to have the money and free time to really enjoy it; films such as *Gone with the Wind* arrived at just the right moment.

In the art deco cathedrals to the moving image that had recently sprung up in town centres, *Gone with the Wind* was open to so many interpretations that it proved capable of casting a spell on just about anyone. Women relished Scarlett O'Hara's transformation from spoilt southern debutante to liberated, spirited Yankee-like entrepreneur. Even though there were no proper battle scenes, men warmed to its sulphurous whiff of bloodshed and bravado. And even though it was screened before the teenage audience had become a breed in itself, teenage girls were transfixed by its heady mixture of patriarchy, romance and Scarlett's stubborn feminism. The whole thing was conceived on such an epic canvas and had such an all-encompassing narrative that it transcended historical romance and became something that everyone could love. Even if its sentimental recreation of the Deep South during the Civil War was told from the perspective of the losing side, in the middle decades of the century it morphed into a distinctively American story of national catastrophe and rebirth, a foundation myth that told the story of America's vision of the world. As much as with Woolworths' expansion during the middle decade of the century, *Gone with the Wind*'s carefully chosen pick 'n' mix of ingredients became an immediate addition to the national heritage, even if the origins of that common inheritance weren't always clear.

Gone with the Wind was a great film because it appealed to everyone, but it was hardly unique. The film critic David Thomson is so enamoured with it that he scripted a documentary about it. When I phoned him at his home in San Francisco, he became immediately wistful for the whole era. 'Between the thirties and the fifties,' he told me, 'there were a slew of films which were made for all ages and which everyone could enjoy, even though people took away different things from them. Those films don't really get made nowadays.' Films like *Gone with the Wind*, *The Wizard of Oz* and *The Philadelphia Story* made sure they were neither too violent nor too disturbing. They were quite happy to cut out any reference to sex to placate the American censors, and while they usually warranted a U certificate on their arrival in the UK, that didn't mean they were simple-minded fare aimed at children. It meant they were for everyone.

Given the power that they had over us, it would scarcely be an exaggeration to say that these films swept us all up and turned us into an audience of the general public, but they couldn't do it on their own. Before it was the biggest film of all time, *Gone with the Wind* was a hugely successful book by Margaret Mitchell, which had been published in 1936. Helped by the success of the film, Mitchell's book would go on to shift an incredible thirty million copies, twenty million of them in a cheap new format called the paperback. Just like the technology for making moving pictures, the equipment for producing these books had been around for nearly half a century, but it was only in the thirties that it was able to find a broad audience. The mass-market paperback was produced to sell in huge numbers and at low prices to ordinary people, but to justify the huge print runs necessary to keep prices low publishers needed to find new – often unconventional – retail outlets in which the general public might find them. In Britain Allen Lane, a director of the Bodley Head publishing house, designed a new size for his proposed paperbacks and assigned different colours for each genre, including the now-iconic orange for fiction, green for crime and dark blue for biographies. He also gave the company's imprint its own name: Penguin. The first ten in his selection appeared in July 1935, and included novels by Mary Webb, Compton Mackenzie and Dorothy L. Sayers as well as Ernest Hemingway's contemporary classic *A Farewell to Arms*. The success of this new venture hinged not only on selecting books that a mass audience might be persuaded to pick up, but on finding an audience. To break even, Lane needed to sell 17,500 copies of each title, and in the months leading up to publication he had been struggling to secure pre-orders for even half of that. In June 1935, however, Allen Lane finally persuaded Woolworths, then growing at an enormous pace, to take a sizeable order. Priced at a very affordable sixpence apiece, the Penguin paperbacks found a home among the sweets, clothes and other goods and the result was to save the Penguin and ignite a revolution in bookselling, bringing books into homes that had never had them before. As well as Woolworths, Allen Lane's books were soon being distributed at airports and train stations in an effort to create a new kind of book-buying public.

Long before Allen Lane's paperback, Penguin had an American competitor in the paperback market. A pioneering former copywriter called Harry Scherman (he would later become a distinguished economist) was convinced that a new market for general books was out there just waiting to be tapped, and that it could best be reached by bypassing traditional bookstores. Allen Lane relied on general retailers to sell his paperbacks, but Scherman had dreamed up a new kind of mail-order distribution. Inaugurated in 1926, the Book-of-the-Month Club promised to bring good books to the masses. To that end, Scherman announced the establishment of a committee of judges or experts, to be made up entirely of paid literary professionals, who would select 'the best new books published each month'. In return for signing up to buy a certain number of books, subscribers would be posted a monthly recommendation arrived at by the judges, which they would be free to send back, together with a catalogue of other books from which they could make their selection. Scherman was initially upbraided by publishers who were worried that he was going to take away their business. Among the public, however, the club was a huge and immediate hit. From an initial list of less than five thousand members in

1926, its subscribers had leapt to sixty thousand by the end of the following year and nearly one hundred thousand by the end of the decade. By 1936 it was so powerful a tastemaker that the publication of *Gone with the Wind* was deliberately held back to coincide with its selection as Book of the Month, a garland that helped enormously in bringing the book to such a massive audience.

Not everyone was happy with the new arrangements. Allen Lane was the subject of a whispering campaign among his fellow publishers, who felt that his efforts were going to ruin the whole industry. When he was accused of making everyone read the same thing, Harry Scherman replied, 'Presumably that's what books are published for.' What both managed to do was to stress how a hand-picked selection of books could be pleasurable and good for the soul. In doing so they conjured up a new kind of book-buyer, a general reader who loves books and could be persuaded to buy them at regular intervals. Just like the big beasts of retail and of Hollywood's studio system, they held us captive and fed us mass-produced slices of stuff which they thought we might like. But what exactly were their ingredients?

Margaret Mitchell's book was neither manufactured pulp nor high art, and many critics seemed not quite sure what to make of it. It was good enough to win a Pulitzer Prize, but even the most generous reviewers felt that its sentimental melodrama didn't quite compare with the literary greats. The film was chivvied along by David O. Selznick, and put together by the best writing and directing team that Hollywood could muster; F. Scott Fitzgerald lent a hand as one of its fifteen screenwriters. It had been put together piece by piece by a huge number of craftsmen, and what one critic called 'the supreme custom-built movie' seemed a little too manufactured to be a work of art. It wasn't long before culture watchers had thought of a quaint new word for it: middlebrow. Middlebrow was a bridge between literary taste and the demands of a mass market. It brought ingredients from high culture and the avant-garde together with the techniques of mass production to serve up a kind of stew that could be appreciated by everyone.

Middlebrow aimed to satisfy the appetite of ordinary people for good stories well told, and was the perfect description of *Gone with the Wind*'s fusion of art, mass production and commerce. The term itself had been around since the twenties, and had recently been popularised by an essay in the 1933 *Review of Literature* by the American poet and novelist Margaret Widdemer. While it was not always easily recognisable in a single work, some critics identified the spread of a kind of corny sentimentality that did its feeling for us and which, lamented the radical art critic Clement Greenberg in his celebrated essay in the *Partisan Review* in 1939, 'predigests art for the spectator and spares him effort'. If middlebrow was difficult to identify in any particular film or book, however, it was much easier to see in the general selection. The kind of 'mid-list' books chosen for the general public by Allen Lane and Harry Scherman were a quintessentially middlebrow amalgam of carefully selected ingredients, pre-digested for the palates of ordinary people by a panel of experts and aimed to raise the general taste. The idea was to cultivate a new kind of general reader; the sort of people who, according to one historian of the Book-of-the-Month Club, 'wanted to be hailed both as intelligent and as broadminded individuals, that is, as lovers of all kinds of books, as aficionados of the universe of print'. In the mainstream media, middlebrow was announced by the rise of magazines like *Reader's Digest*. It could also be seen in the way that newspapers extended their breadth and their reach beyond business and politics to cover matters of general interest. In the brave new world of broadcast television, middlebrow's best ambassador was Lord Reith, the first director general of the British Broadcasting Corporation, who announced a pick 'n' mix mission to 'inform, educate and entertain' an audience of millions. The middlebrow centrepiece of American television was *Omnibus*, a weekly ninety-minute summary of developments in science, arts and the humanities that played on the three major American TV networks to seventeen million viewers between 1952 and 1961. In the programme's brochure, which was used to tout for sponsorship and sell their audience to advertisers, the producers were very clear about what they hoped to achieve. *Omnibus* would, they said, 'be aimed straight at the average American audience, neither highbrow nor lowbrow . . . but the audience that made the great circulations of such magazines as *Reader's Digest*, *Life*, the *Ladies' Home Journal*, the audience which is the solid backbone of any business as it is of America itself.' It was to be a pick 'n' mix, in other words, an edifying assortment of quality viewing general enough to have something for everyone.

There was one more reason why *Gone with the Wind* chimed with the American psyche in the thirties, and why sellers of everything from films to books to household goods were able to find such a broad audience for their wares. In the middle of that decade western societies began to emerge from a biting economic depression, and what helped them to do so was an historic bargain forged between political elites and the masses. In the United States it was symbolised by the New Deal, the package of economic assistance sponsored by President Franklin D. Roosevelt, while in Britain it was the onset of a war economy and tentative moves in the directions of a welfare state. When those programmes for social insurance were fully implemented following the Second World War, the consequences were to raise wages, shrink the working week and send huge numbers of young people into the higher education system. With more money and more free time at their disposal, people could be persuaded to shop and spend money, and the big beasts of retail and popular culture were soon reaping the benefits. By the early fifties Harry Scherman's Book-of-the-Month Club had over half a million subscribers, and Allen Lane's paperback imprint had taken such a chunk out of the market that Penguin had become synonymous with the word paperback. Bookshelves in living rooms everywhere heaved with a selection of wholesome-looking volumes, even if many of them remained unread.

People also had more time for politics. Thanks to the Representation of the People Act 1928, for example, ordinary British men and women were now extended the right to vote. Voting, however, was only mass production extended into the realm of politics, and if all those millions of votes were going to add up to a popular franchise they needed to be arranged in such a way that they made sense. In the nineteenth century, political parties had been organised in local caucuses, most of which were fairly independent of each other. By the middle of the twentieth century, however, a new kind of political party had sprung up in most democracies, one that scooped up local associations, trade unions and church groups into formidable national machines. Writing in 1951, Maurice Duverger was able to claim that 'the structure of parties has been completely transformed' in the previous half-century, and to confidently predict that the mass-membership political party was becoming the party of the future. By the early fifties, individual membership of the two major British political parties had reached an unprecedented peak. In the few years following the Second World War, membership of the British Conservative party alone had leapt from just under one million to over two and three-quarters.

Political parties were on the way to becoming big beasts, gobbling up millions of ordinary people and integrating them into the body politic. Just as films like *Gone with the Wind* helped galvanise us into a national culture, so political parties bound us into national democracies and gave everyone a stake in the running of government. In the same way in which the big beasts of retail and cinema had a monopoly on the products that they sold, ambitious politicians soon discovered that mainstream political parties had a monopoly over access to political jobs; that they were the only vehicle for selection to political office. And, just as the middlebrow had formed a bridge between literary and mass-market taste, the growth of mainstream political parties threw up a consensus on the kinds of things that politicians should argue about, and a coherent range of policies – again, a kind of pick 'n' mix – from which the voters could choose. By forging this link between those in charge and the popular mood, they succeeded in carving out a congenial middle ground. They had become the only show in town, and we were their grateful audience.

3

Nonetheless, that audience wasn't just going to roll up on its own. It needed to be assembled, teased, chivvied, seduced and finally mobilised. Returning to *Gone with the Wind*, an early example of what could be done to this end was the work of the film's producer, David O. Selznick, No sooner had Selznick bought the rights to the book than he announced a nationwide talent search to find the perfect Scarlett, and held a press conference to trumpet the news that three top talent executives would be assigned to different regions of the country. The public were to be fully involved, their views were solicited via polls, newspaper stories and fan magazines; the whole process would take two years, would cost ninety-two thousand dollars and would create so much interest that fourteen thousand candidates presented themselves for the role of Scarlett. Fans wrote in with their suggestions, astrologers offered their advice and a procession of wannabe Scarletts took it upon themselves to show up at Selznick's Beverley Hills home for an impromptu screen test. Nothing came of it, but that wasn't the point. Selznick was simply putting together an audience for a film that hadn't even been made. His extended drumroll for *Gone with the Wind* was an audacious effort, but it lacked sophistication. The big beasts had successfully captured the attention of the general public but if they were going to feed it and keep it happy they needed to know a little more about it and what it wanted to eat. To help them out, they engaged the services of a flashy new kind of social scientist whose job it was to poke the general public and monitor its behaviour, to ask it what it was thinking and to figure out how it felt.

In 1937 Mass-Observation, a wholly new social research organisation, was established with the aim of studying the everyday habits and behaviour of the British public. One of its founders, Tom Harrisson, was a keen bird-watcher and naturalist, and his training might well have inspired some of the techniques honed by Mass-Observation. From Harrisson's base in Bolton, records John Carey in his book *The Intellectuals and the Masses*, five hundred volunteer observers were sent out to mingle among the natives and quietly report back on local customs such as 'football pools, dirty jokes, armpit hygiene and the proportion of males wearing bowler hats in pubs. Observers were instructed to use an impersonal notation when identifying human specimens.' By the fifties, their reports were being mulled over by everyone from market researchers to the British government.

It was in this decade, too, that an American statistician called George Gallup fine-tuned his whizzy new survey-sampling techniques. Gallup had started out measuring public opinion on behalf of advertisers; in 1938 he consolidated his different polling agencies in a single organisation and began to take the temperature of the American public at regular intervals. There was no shortage of people qualified to interpret the data of the Gallup polls. 'Fortunately for the ad men,' revealed Vance Packard in *The Hidden Persuaders*, his best-selling 1957 exposé of the methods of the American advertising industry, 'the supply of social scientists to draw from had multiplied in profusion within the decade. There were for example now at least seven thousand accredited psychologists. At first the ad men had a hard time getting straight in their own mind the various types of social scientists. They were counselled that sociologists and anthropologists were concerned with people in groups, whereas psychologists and psychiatrists were mainly concerned with what goes on in the mind of the individual.' By 1960 there were so many clipboard-carrying pollsters, psephologists, pop sociologists and public relations gurus prowling for information about the American public that the critic Dwight MacDonald railed against the rise of what he termed 'questionnaire sociologists', who saw citizens as little more than statistics in skins. The problem with the professional people-watchers, he argued, was that they 'degrade the public by treating it as an object, to be handled with the lack of ceremony of medical students dissecting a corpse, and at the same time flatter it and pander to its taste and ideas by taking them as the criterion of reality'.

MacDonald was right to assume that the big beasts had ambitious plans for what to do with all this data at their disposal. Some, for example, began to use it to segment their customers by income, geography, gender and education – the better to sell them more stuff. One of the first companies to figure out how to do this was General Motors. By 1930, along with the other two car-makers in Detroit's big three, Ford and Chrysler, GM had a captive audience of millions of Americans for its vehicles. But whereas Henry Ford had sold his Model T as the cheapest, most basic transportation vehicle that mass production would allow ('Any customer can have a car painted any colour that he wants,' Ford famously bragged, 'so long as it is black'), in the late twenties Alfred Sloan, president of General Motors, decided that his company would offer something altogether more classy: a variety of different quality cars, from which they could pick and choose according to their income bracket. Each car would start life on the same production line, but the various models would then be shipped off to different locations to be worked on and finished off.

The imperious Sloan had been born into a prosperous New York family and liked the idea of giving the common man something worth aspiring to. His plan was to present car-buyers with a 'ladder of success' that they could ascend as they found the wherewithal to do so. Forty years later, in his autobiography *My Years with General Motors*, Sloan explained how it was supposed to work:

> The Cadillac and the Buick were first and second from the top of the price pyramid. The Chevrolet was always the base of the pyramid. The Oakland organization, which produced the Pontiac car, later became the Pontiac division, and the manufacture of Oakland cars was discontinued. The Pontiac became a distinctive car in its own right while maintaining its original economies. That put Olds between Pontiac and Buick, making the basic line: Chevrolet, Pontiac, Olds, Buick, and Cadillac, more or less as it is today.

Sure enough, Sloan's brilliant strategy of dividing GM's audience into income bands became the company's magic ingredient, its secret sauce. It helped General Motors race past Ford to become the world's biggest car maker in the thirties, and it would go on to fuel much of the company's growth and international expansion for the next three decades. In 1954 GM was selling more than half of all the cars sold in America, and plenty more via its British arm Vauxhall and its German subsidiary Opel. Sleek new models like the Chevy Camaro were as eagerly anticipated as iPhones. So deep were the company's pockets that for an entire decade it paid for an exclusive sponsorship deal with *Bonanza*, the Western TV series and then one of America's most popular family shows, just so it could introduce each episode with a celebrity behind the wheel of one of its cars singing along to ditties like 'See the USA in your Chevrolet'. By the beginning of the sixties General Motors had become as much a symbol of America's industrial might as Hollywood was testament to its mastery of popular culture.

It was in this decade, however, that the control of the big beasts showed the first signs of loosening. As the welfare state grew and more of its initiatives could be seen to serve the interests of everyone, the common interests that tied people into trade unions began to look narrow and self-interested, kicking against the whole system. Then there were the social convulsions of the late sixties, in which a fresh generation of protesters did their utmost to break free of the big beasts and their definition of what the public wanted. The result was to make allegiances and loyalties less predictable to pollsters of any kind, and to shake the confidence of the big beasts. A new species of voter, known as a floating voter or swing voter, bubbled to the surface of the political system, and didn't want to be tied down to any particular party. The German-American Otto Kirchheimer was one of the first scholars to notice that anything was amiss. He observed in the mid-sixties that the two main political parties in West Germany, the centre-right Christian Democratic Union (CDU) and the centre-left Social Democratic Party (SPD), had recently dropped their ideological baggage and made for the centre ground. Rather than speaking to their traditional constituencies, the German parties had, according to Kirchheimer, morphed into catch-all parties that deliberately opened themselves as wide as they could in order to scoop up the burgeoning shoals of floating voters whose allegiances were up for grabs.

At least in the short term, the strategy seemed to work. By the early seventies, West Germany's two big parties shared 90 per cent of the vote and political parties everywhere, Kirchheimer predicted, would soon be tempted to follow suit. But which direction should they swim in to order to scoop up the most votes? In 1957 an inventive young political scientist called Anthony Downs came up with an ingenious answer. In the short but hugely influential *An Economic Theory of Democracy*, Downs pointed out that if everyone in the voting population could be lined up on a single left-right axis according to their political outlook, it would be very easy to identify the voter in the middle – what he termed the 'median voter'. Downs was not referring to the arithmetic mean, which could be had by adding up all the votes and dividing by the number of voters. He was talking about the average voter, but only in the sense that every single voter could be lined up according to their views and the one in the middle identified with some precision. Political parties hungry for power, Downs concluded, would be well advised to pin everything on chasing this median voter.

The rise of catch-all parties and their drift towards the median voter was followed keenly by political parties everywhere. For many political scientists, Downs's logic helps explain why most modern American presidential candidates, once they have courted their party loyalists in the primaries, usually head with unseemly haste in the direction of the centre ground. The thrust of Downs's argument, however, went far beyond its usefulness to politicians. His logic could be traced back to Harold Hotelling's 1929 article in the *Economic Journal*. In any audience or population distribution, Hotelling posited, the best way to broaden one's appeal and achieve maximum reach would be to ply one's wares right at the middle, and anyone who didn't was likely to be defeated by those who did. Imagine an ice-cream seller who has to decide where to set up shop on a beach-front where holidaymakers are evenly distributed along the beach. To have the best chance of touting his wares to the greatest number of customers, Hotelling's law dictates that he should set up his ice-cream stand exactly in the middle of the beach-front. But that wasn't all. When a second ice-cream seller pitches up to offer the first a little competition he should, following the same logic, set up shop back to back with the first ice-cream seller rather than at the end of the beach, where he would only attract custom from one side. The argument seems counterintuitive, but as big beasts of all kinds found their once loyal customers floating away it wasn't only political parties who found it compelling. By drilling down into the data, after all, it would be very easy to ask their hired statistical hands to line up audiences according to their income, politics or anything else and use that information to identify the middle ground. Then, a bit like those two ice-cream sellers, all they would need to do was to pitch up there as fast as they could.

4

In the early eighties, by the time I was watching *Gone with the Wind*, its era was already drawing to a close. Feminists including Gloria Steinem had complained about the infamous 'rape' scene in which Rhett Butler manhandles Scarlett up a staircase to have his way with her, while civil rights activists like Alice Walker had taken exception to its blatantly racist portrayal of black slaves as happy simpletons. *Gone with the Wind* still counts as the highest-grossing film ever made, when adjusted for inflation, but it was not really a blockbuster. If blockbuster is defined as a kind of film rather than the size of its box office takings, its origins are usually dated to 20 June 1975 and the arrival of *Jaws*. For the Hollywood studios, the killer shark arrived not a moment too soon. Just like many other big beasts, their sureness of touch had been slipping away since the late sixties, when the aftershock of a decade of social rebellion sent ripples through the population and made its appetite less easy to predict. All of a sudden Hollywood moguls didn't seem to know who their audience was, or how to satisfy it. In 1971, *Variety* magazine announced that an historic low of 15.8 million Americans bothered to go to the cinema on a weekly basis. Not only that, but an iconoclastic new generation of directors like Martin Scorsese had inveigled its way into Hollywood and didn't seem to care much about audiences at all.

For the studios, then, *Jaws* was their great white hope. It was a new kind of film. It was directed by the man who would go on to become the David O. Selznick of his day, Steven Spielberg, and it opened simultaneously in so many hundreds of cinemas across America that it could hardly fail to make money. Whereas *Gone with the Wind* had opened relatively quietly in December 1939, *Jaws* and all the blockbusters that followed were made specifically for summer launches, when they could be sure to find a broad audience of teenagers and their parents. While it drew on the paranoia pervasive in the films of Martin Scorsese and Robert De Niro, says the film historian Peter Biskind in his book *Easy Riders, Raging Bulls*, its intention was to be 'no longer narrowly and tendentiously defined as the hip counterculture, but . . . expansive and inclusive, a new community comprised of just about everyone.' Just like its great white star, in other words, *Jaws* opened its mouth as wide as it could to gobble up the greatest possible audience.

The problem was that, having worked up an appetite for summer blockbusters, the Hollywood studios didn't know when to stop. The studios became hooked on the massive marketing and merchandising campaigns that went along with their push into cinemas, and before long the new cinema multiplexes that had appeared on the outskirts of towns in the eighties were on the receiving end of a grim conveyor belt of formulaic and instantly forgettable film franchises. In 1989, to take a single year, cinemagoers could choose from among *Lethal Weapon 2*, *Ghostbusters II*, *The Karate Kid, Part III*, *Back to the Future Part II*, *A Nightmare on Elm Street 5*, *Star Trek V*, *Friday the 13th Part VIII* and *Police Academy 6*. Sometimes the exception proved the rule. One of the last times an original Hollywood film appeared which could with reasonable certainty be said to appeal to all age groups, it was James Cameron's *Titanic* in 1998. Here was film-making on *Gone with the Wind*'s epic scale, combining sentimental melodrama with state-of-the-art effects, and the finished spectacle proved unsinkable – *Titanic* took six hundred million dollars at the box office, more even than *Star Wars* or *E.T.*, and became the most successful film of its era. Just like *Gone with the Wind*, *Titanic* opened in a chilly December so as to reach beyond the teenage audience. Its reception was one of the last occasions when the views of the film-making academy agreed with those of the film-going audience: the film landed fourteen Oscar nominations and came away with eleven of them. But it was a dying breed. In the year of its release, Bill Mechanic, the chief executive of Twentieth Century Fox who had overseen its production, lamented the fact that films like it were on the way out:

> When you had *Gone with the Wind*, the system was much more controlled. Movies were 90 per cent of leisure time activities. Movies are now probably 10 per cent, so you're fighting a confluence of other media . . . The attempt to break through that kind of clutter, and reach the most number of people, had undercut the process. The idea had taken over from the movie itself. They look like movies and they sound like movies and they feel like 'em until you get inside 'em and then that lack of caring shows.

Mechanic meant that the cinema had lost its monopoly on the attention of the film-going audience and had been on a long downhill road ever since. In some ways, however, he and his fellow movie bosses only had themselves to blame. Even *Titanic* had been aimed squarely at the average viewer, and its director James Cameron growled at the majority of critics who craved films 'far too refined for the average individual to possibly appreciate'. But as movie moguls all vied to locate that average viewer and scoop up the audience, their summertime blockbusters nose-dived towards the lowest common denominator. The film industry's big beasts had become like the ice-cream sellers, piling en masse towards the middle of the beach-front because it was the only way they could look out over the whole of the beach.

They weren't the only ones. By the late seventies executives at General Motors were unnerved to discover that a relatively new arrival in the American market, the Japanese company Toyota, was eating into their customer base with high-quality cars which were usually lighter and better made than their own. Like the other big beasts of the Detroit car industry, GM was at first dismissive of the threat to their natural monopoly over the American car-buyer and found reasons to ignore it. When that didn't work, GM became defensive, cutting costs to protect its share of the market. To do so it resorted to a new kind of production called 'badge engineering'. What badge engineering meant was that instead of building wholly new models for its range of cars, the company would do more of the work on its different models on the same production line from the same parts and then rebadge them with different wheels, grilles and colours; underneath the paintwork, they would be almost exactly the same. It was an understandable move. 'You have to have common platforms to make cars,' says Aaron Bragman, a Michigan-based car industry analyst who has been following the fortunes of General Motors for many years, 'otherwise most of them would work out too expensive to make. But badge engineering took things much further and minimised the differences between their different models. The thought was that the end customer shouldn't really notice the difference.' As competition at home heated up, GM kept devouring international brands. In the course of the nineties, for example, it gobbled up Saab, the Swedish firm with a reputation for making stylish and svelte cars, and Hummer, which had made its name with heavy, fortress-like trucks and sports-utility vehicles. Before long General Motors was responsible for twelve different car brands, but with so many brands to manage and so many costs to shave, it struggled to produce enough models to keep fans of those cars happy. Even worse, its managers brought badge engineering to many of its new acquisitions – making Saab Sports Utility Vehicles, for example, which looked suspiciously like those they had been selling back home under their own General Motors labels.

The rungs of the company's once well-defined ladder of brands were no longer clear. Instead, the various brands hovered around the middle ground both in terms of their quality and how much they cost, making it difficult to distinguish a Chevy from a Pontiac or a Buick. By steering all of its different brands to converge in the middle of the road, the company had squandered everything that made them different. By the turn of the new millennium General Motors was unravelling. The ladder that was supposed to lift its buyers through its various brands came tumbling down amid swingeing corporate losses. For the industry-watchers who had seen it coming, it was all deeply frustrating. 'The whole point,' Aaron Bragman told me, 'was that the customer was supposed to see progress along a ladder of the different brands, but the cars ended up so alike that they sucked all the life out of them.' The irony, he says, is that the Chevrolet is now better made than it has been for many decades, but customers remain to be convinced: 'Trying to get Americans back into the fold of GM is going to be extremely difficult, because the damage has been done.'

The General Motors of the food and drink industry was General Foods, though as a result of a series of mergers and name-changes in the last few decades, it now trades under the name Kraft. In its heyday General Foods gave America some of its most treasured mainstream brands, like Maxwell House coffee. Maxwell House first became famous during the Second World War, when instant coffee powder was popular among American troops serving overseas. By the time they arrived home it had become one of America's most loved brands. Over the next few decades, along with its rivals Folgers and Hill Bros, Maxwell House consolidated control of American coffee consumption.

It was during those same years, however, that the quality of its coffee went downhill. It wasn't difficult to work out why. There are two kinds of coffee beans: Arabica and Robusta. Arabica beans have the finest aroma and make for the most flavoursome coffee. Since they are also vulnerable to weather fluctuations and attacks from parasites, they are more expensive to grow. Robusta beans, as their name suggests, are more resilient, which makes them cheaper. The problem is that they usually produce a bitter and vastly inferior taste. Following a terrible frost that wiped out almost all of the Brazilian coffee crop in 1953, the price of Arabica soared. Maxwell House and the other major

American roasters responded by adding a little more Robusta to their blend. No one seemed to notice, and so the next time a coffee crop failed they added a little more.

To make sure they weren't losing any business, Maxwell House organised taste tests that purported to show that coffee-drinkers couldn't tell the difference. But, while the profits of the major roasters continued to look healthy, and instant coffee was accounting for 90 per cent of all retail coffee sales, coffee drinkers were quietly going elsewhere. In the sixties, young Americans began to desert coffee for soft drinks such as Coca-Cola and Pepsi. Between 1962 and 1974, says Mark Pendergrast in his book *Uncommon Grounds*, American coffee consumption per capita dropped from 3.12 cups a day to 2.25 cups. Once again, the American coffee giants responded by adding more Robusta to further reduce their costs. They also spent heavily on television advertisements. One 1978 campaign featured an elderly general-store owner named Cora insisting that she only saw fit to stock Maxwell House. 'When you only got room for one brand,' she told millions of American viewers, 'it's a mighty easy choice. Like they say, it's good to the last drop.' Their choice of actress was a little eccentric: viewers might have dimly recognised that the genial Cora was Margaret Hamilton, who was known chiefly for having played the Wicked Witch of the West in *The Wizard of Oz*. When a rival coffee company replied with a homely storekeeper of its own, one television critic denounced 'the battle of the old bags'. It didn't work. Americans were slowly losing the habit of drinking instant coffee. In 1975, after another frost in Brazil laid waste to the Arabica crop, all the major roasters added yet more Robusta. A decade later, in 1985, Maxwell House went back to the drawing board again, adding even more bitter Robusta to its blend. By the mid-nineties it was clear that the big roasters who controlled the American coffee industry had given up producing a quality product and were competing in a headlong race to the bottom. For all the advertising dollars lavished on it, their coffee tasted like tar.

The adjustments that General Foods and then Kraft made to its Maxwell House blend are known to industry insiders as 'value engineering'. Value engineering, like badge engineering, involves tinkering with a product to keep down the costs of producing it. If many of the mainstream products you fondly remember from your youth seem to have shrunk as you've grown up, value engineering means that they probably have. Sometimesit means no more than quietly shaving a little weight off the product – it is value engineering, for example, that explains why, in 2008, Nestlé removed the eleventh Rolo from a packet, and why in the same year Cadbury's shrank their Dairy Milk bar from 250 grams to 230 grams. More often, however, it involves cutting the cost of the ingredients. Take another Kraft product, its macaroni cheese ready meal. Reputedly invented by a St Louis salesman in 1937, Kraft Macaroni & Cheese has since become one of America's most familiar products and the archetypal comfort food. Just like Maxwell House, it is steeped in nostalgia: the orangey dish came into its own during the Second World War, when shoppers realised they could buy two boxes of it in return for a single ration stamp. In the late nineties, however, threatened with competition from supermarket own-brand competitors, Kraft's managers and food scientists began to play around with the ingredients and manufacturing processes. With cost savings of 2 or 3 per cent to achieve every year, they had to be creative: instead of the dried cheddar and buttermilk formula they used prior to 1997, for example, they began to use a lower-cost cheese culture. 'If you look at the list of ingredients on a box of their current product,' noted the retail analysts Michael J. Silverstein and John Butman in their 2006 book *Treasure Hunt*, 'you'll see that there is no "real" cheese on the list. That's probably because real cheese is expensive. The product is now made with cheese culture, whey, milk fat, milk protein concentrate, salt, calcium carbonate, sodium tripolyphosphate and other ingredients. The package says that Kraft Macaroni & Cheese is "the cheesiest," and many consumers still seem to like the taste. But if you were able to compare it to Kraft Macaroni & Cheese made in 1997, which was made with "real" dried cheddar cheese and buttermilk, you could probably taste the difference.'

In July 2007 Kraft finally reformulated its Maxwell House to include only Arabica beans. In the same year, a spokesperson for the company told me, it made a 'quality improvement' to its Macaroni & Cheese by adding 'even more cheese'. Kraft still sells more than a million of the ready meals every day in the United States, and the product is still hugely profitable. Paring away at its ingredients over the years, however, has left it exposed. Whatever else it was between 1997 and 2007, Kraft's Macaroni & Cheese is unlikely to have been 'the cheesiest'. Even now, Wal-Mart or Safeway's macaroni and cheese dinner is cheaper and probably just as good; Wal-Mart own-brand version, according to the list of ingredients on the side of the packet, is made with real cheddar cheese. In a 2010 Nielsen survey, more than 60 per cent of Americans said they couldn't see any difference between branded products and the kind of own-label goods available in supermarkets and discount stores. At some point over the last two decades, it seems, many of the mainstream brands we know and love have become indistinguishable from their own-brand competitors. Just like the cars from General

Motors and many of the films from Hollywood's major studios, they've begun to look generic.

5

Faced with threats to their position and with their audiences slipping away, many of the big beasts who gave us our mainstream products spread themselves very thin. They wanted to draw in as big an audience as they could, as cheaply as possible. Even if it worked in the short term by reducing their costs, it damaged their reputation for quality. It made them difficult to distinguish from each other and their competitors.

As shoppers spend more time in shopping malls and in supermarkets, it's left them even more vulnerable. Just a few yards away from where I live on London's Old Kent Road is a branch of the supermarket Tesco. It's a huge store – it's name is Tesco Southwark, as if it were big enough to cater for an entire London borough – and once inside you can buy just about anything you might want on your weekly shop. Not only is there a huge range of produce, but there's a wide variety of different options and prices within each product category: Tesco's value range, a broad selection of mainstream brands and then Tesco Finest, its high-end range of luxury food and drink. Next door to Tesco is The 99p store, a plucky local discounter specialising in selling a small number of products at a single rock-bottom price; in an impoverished inner-city area, it does a healthy trade.

A supermarket like Tesco Southwark is popular because it is big enough to stock almost everything. Think of it as an ecosystem: it works by creating an environment in which shoppers are free to range around and find anything that they want at the price that they want it. Mid-range, branded brands like Maxwell House were traditionally seen as guarantees of quality and reliability, in return for which those who bought them were happy to pay a little extra. They got used to taking pride of place on the store shelf, but now they've been plunged into a new kind of retail landscape in which they're forced to share shelf space. In this new environment many mainstream brands aren't cheap enough to warrant being bought for their price alone, but nor are they of appreciably higher quality than the own-brand products that sit beside them. Neither exceptionally good nor exceptionally cheap, it is difficult know why we should single them out. They're stuck in the middle.

This hole in the middle of the market can be seen not only in the range of products on supermarket shelves, but in the range of shops that house them. Even before the recession, an almost Darwinian struggle was laying waste to our high streets. Thinking about the changing high street made me wonder how the view from my front door on the Old Kent Road looked before Tesco arrived, and one day I went to a nearby local history library to find out. In a large steel cabinet I discovered a file of illustrations and pictures of how the row of shops directly opposite my house had changed over the centuries. There had been confectioners, granaries, lingerie shops, butchers, shoe shops, greengrocers, ironmongers, pubs, tobacconists, florists, chemists, milliners and fashion shops. A folder of black-and-white photographs taken in 1978 shows that many of them had sold up, that they'd given way to now-forgotten department stores such as House of Holland and Coopers. In the middle of the row, right where Tesco now stands at 325 Old Kent Road, was Woolworths; in the accompanying post office directory, it proudly identified itself as a bazaar. Just a few years later, however, the ground would collapse beneath it and it would become a part of a larger retail ecosystem. It must have been one of the first Woolworths to go, but it wouldn't be the last.

The response of Woolies to competition from the supermarkets, as we've seen, was to expand its range to encourage more people through the door. As it spread itself thinner, over a wider selection of goods, it was gravitating towards what it hoped would be the safe middle ground. It didn't work. Woolworths was never going to be a supermarket. Even if stocking a wider range of stuff worked in the short term by shoring up sales, it took its toll on the store's reputation for quality, its authority over the things that it sold. Whereas the big beasts of manufacturing were tempted to water down the ingredients of their products, Woolworths was tempted to water down its range. In the end, the things in its stores were neither very cheap nor very distinctive – there seemed little reason for them to be there, and there was very little in its stores that you couldn't find anywhere else. Woolworths was caught in the middle of the market, and eventually it was bulldozed out of the way.

As we'll see later, the masses of information on the internet make it even easier to cut a swath through the middle in search of either outstanding value or quality. Long before we began to spend time online, however, department stores like Woolworths were suffering at the hands of supermarkets and value stores. In 1970 Woolworths had been America's fourth-largest retailer, but by 2004 it was extinct in that country. (The Australian company Woolworths, which has no connection to the company founded by Frank Woolworth, has found one way around the problem by getting rid of its general stores and remaking them as huge food supermarkets: it's now the biggest supermarket chain in both Australia and New Zealand.) Woolworths isn't the only store to have come up against the missing middle. In 1970 Sears Roebuck was America's biggest retailer, but by 2004 it was only ninth; JCPenney was in second place in 1970, but by 2004 it had fallen back to sixteenth.

Just like Woolworths, mid-range, mid-market retailers now find themselves under attack from all directions. And, just like Woolworths, many have been tempted to head for the very middle of the middle market, either by focusing more narrowly on middle-aged customers or by expanding their range. Since the late seventies, British retailers such as Marks & Spencer, Next and Debenhams have been taking business away from Woolworths in food, clothes and household goods, but in the last decade they too have found themselves in the exposed middle ground caught between bargain retailers on the one hand and premium stores on the other. In clothes and homewares, for example, both Next and Debenhams are being squeezed by cheaper stores like H&M, Zara and Ikea, while Marks & Spencer is threatened by the high-end supermarket Waitrose. In November 2009 Marks & Spencer announced that, for the first time in eighty-five years, it would begin selling popular household staples like Coca-Cola and Heinz beans alongside its own produce so that so that its customers could get all their essentials in one shop. In March of the following year, its outgoing chairman Sir Stuart Rose told a conference that he'd like to see even more of these branded products in M&S stores. 'Tesco is a good example of a brand that says . . . we will sell you anything you can think of. At M&S, we haven't traditionally done that . . . I haven't a clue why not.' One reason why not is that it might damage the store's reputation for quality. When I asked a cashier in my local M&S what her regular customers made of the arrival of KitKats and other branded chocolate bars in front of her till, she told me that many seemed pleased to see them. Others, though, were a little put out: 'They're saying it's just not Marks & Spencer.' Marc Bolland, the incoming CEO of Marks & Spencer, seemed to agree. In an embarrassing about-turn in November 2010, Bolland abandoned the supermarket idea and drastically reduced the number of non-M&S foodstuffs in its stores; the company, he said, need to refocus itself around a more international, specialist niche.

At around the same time, something similar happened to bookselling. In the course of the eighties and nineties, the small independent bookstores that had once ruled the roost were steamrolled by the spread of chains such as Barnes & Noble and Borders in the United States and Waterstone's in the UK who took to selling books at a significant discount. In the fifteen years between 1991 and 2005, according to the American Booksellers Association, the number of independent bookstores declined by two thirds, from 5200 to 1702. This was not necessarily a bad thing. With greater buying power than a small independent bookshop, a chain store like Waterstone's, which specialised in selling literary fiction and quality non-fiction, had the muscle to build the careers of promising writers. As the book chains expanded beyond small metropolitan audiences, however, they found that they needed to expand the range of books that they sold and standardise their book-buying at head office. Not only that but, beset by rising rents, competition from supermarkets and online retailers and demands for greater profits from the huge conglomerates into whose laps they had sometimes dropped, the book chains were soon asking local managers to give over more space to the kind of mass-market blockbusters that lacked literary merit but whose vast sales helped pay the bills. The result was to suck away shelf-space from the kind of middlebrow fare that booksellers liked to stock but which didn't tend to sell in huge numbers. Publishers, too, began to compete with each other for the privilege of publishing endlessly formulaic, infinitely disposable books that drew attention away from the rest of their list. More books than ever are now being published, but the share of the market taken by bestsellers appears to be on the inexorable rise. Sales of the ten best-selling books in Britain leapt from 3.4 million to 6 million between 1998 and 2008; even though 120,000 authors sold books in 2008, according to data published in the *Bookseller*, the top fifty accounted for a massive £250 million worth of business.

Faced with increasing competition and the need to cut costs, general-interest publishers and booksellers chose to open their mouths wide and gobble everyone up in search of the average customer. Doing so helped shore up their balance sheet for a time, but it also played havoc with their reputation for feeding their audience a nutritious diet of general-interest books. When mainstream, middlebrow literature had opened its clutches to include almost everything, it didn't really seem to stand for anything. Neither did Harry Scherman's defiantly middlebrow Book-of-the-Month Club. By the eighties it was already under huge pressure from chain bookstores that had the purchasing power to buy books in greater numbers and sell them more cheaply than ever before. Then there was the rise of TV-based book clubs like Oprah Winfrey's in the United States and Richard and Judy's in the UK, which were sometimes very good at presenting difficult books to their audiences but didn't have the same authority or exclusive hold over their audiences as mail-order book clubs. The Book-of-the-Month Club fired its illustrious panel of judges in 1994 and, in an attempt to cut its costs and focus on the bottom line, it began to lean more heavily on blockbuster authors like Tom Clancy and Robert Ludlum. 'The BOMC has gone the way of the British royal family and other preposterous pleasures,' complained one former judge, the writer Wilfrid Sheed. 'With the growth of the so-called best-seller mentality,' a former executive at the company observed, what has changed 'is the publishing industry's ability to design books that might appeal to people who ordinarily read only magazines and newspapers or who watch television.' By 2004 membership of the Book-of-the-Month Club was seven hundred thousand, less than half of what it had been just fifteen years earlier. Book groups were sprouting up all over the United States, and unprecedented millions of Americans were involved in them, but membership of the Book-of-the-Month Club was foundering. It had lost control of its audience and, when it responded by watering down its pick 'n' mix of literary ingredients, it surrendered its reputation for ensuring that the best books rose to the top.

Underlying all this, then, was a deeper problem. In heading for the middle ground in search of the average consumer, the big beasts of retail were only trying to scoop up the biggest possible audience available to them. Doing so, however, only made it even more difficult to win the allegiance of any particular constituency. Mainstream political parties have encountered much the same problem. By the time I came to study and then teach politics in the mid-nineties, Anthony Down's suggestion to head for the median voter seemed to have become the only game in town. Political parties that tried to widen their appeal in this way soon discovered that even if they could swallow a shoal of floating voters in one election they would very likely have escaped by the time it came for the next. In the German elections of 2005, for example, the two major catch-all political parties, the Christian Democrats and the Social Democrats, took less than 70 per cent of the vote, their lowest combined score since 1949. The result was to force them into a 'grand coalition', which only made it more difficult to tell them apart.

Many political parties had seen their membership hollowed out by the same kind of logic. Since their zenith of popularity in the fifties, for example, the two major British political parties, Labour and Conservative, have been in a relentless spiral of decline. Between the beginning of the sixties and the end of the eighties, the percentage of the British electorate marshalled in mainstream political parties fell from 9.4 per cent to 3.3 per cent. When Tony Blair won the leadership of the Labour party in July 1994, he mounted a spirited battle to reverse the tide. For the first four years his campaign to recruit new party members looked like a stroke of genius, and succeeded in swelling party membership by 40 per cent. There was a problem, however, in that most of the new arrivals felt no real affinity with the Labour Party, and most of them resigned their membership soon after the party entered government in 1997. From a relative peak of 405,000 in that year, according to figures it submitted to the Electoral Commission, membership of the British Labour Party fell to 156,000 in 2010.

*

The big beasts of retail, media and politics now find themselves in an unenviable position. Many of them hove into view only in the middle decades of the twentieth century, and only thanks to a unique confluence of history, politics and the appearance of new industrial machinery – a set of circumstances that are now on their way out. By holding us captive with a near-monopoly over our attention, they integrated the general public into a broad new kind of culture. Little by little, however, the vehicle in which they held us – from the pick 'n' mix display in department stores to the selection of policies offered us by mainstream political parties, from the middlebrow films produced by Hollywood to the midlist fare on offer in the Book-of-the-Month Club – broke down. Mainstream institutions that still aim to serve up a quality selection of ingredients for a general audience now find themselves embattled. Some, like the BBC, are enduring brickbats and humiliation from all around. Others have responded to falling profits, rising rents and disappearing audiences by opening their mouths wide and piling towards the very middle of the middle ground. In practice, that has often meant cutting losses and reaching for the lowest common denominator. For many, what started out as a pick 'n' mix selection of quality fare aimed at the general public has come to look more like an expensive jumble sale. Even if it worked to shore up their profits in the short term, it has left audiences with no real affinity with them, no way of distinguishing one institution from another.

Sinking to the bottom wasn't the only answer. The market for good coffee, for example, never entirely went away. In the years after the Second World War it was kept alive in big-city coffee houses, where the conscientious Italian owners took to using expensive Gaggia machines to produce espresso-based brews of the highest quality. In the seventies, an indigenous coffee house movement sprung up on America's West Coast, inviting coffee enthusiasts to buy freshly roasted beans and drink good coffee on their premises. Each gourmet coffee store had its own style and roasting preferences but one, a Seattle-based company called Starbucks, stood out.

Starbucks had started life in 1971 but its epiphany came when its then sales manager Howard Schultz, on a buying trip in Milan, fell in love with Italian coffee culture and the brio that baristas brought to serving up an excellent cup of coffee. Back home in Seattle, he and other Starbucks executives set about trying to recreate that experience for an American audience. They gave the company's beverages new, cod-Italian names to make the consumer sound like a connoisseur: the larger couple sizes, for example, became grande and venti. 'It's amazing to me that these terms have become part of the language,' Dawn Pinaud, a former Starbucks executive, told the writer Mark Pendergrast when interviewed for *Uncommon Grounds*. 'A few of us sat in a conference room and just made them up.' Starbucks wanted to attract enthusiasts who could be persuaded to pay handsomely in return for genuinely high-quality coffee. These aficionados would be looking for fine Arabica beans, of course, but they'd want more than that. Since each coffee-growing region produces beans with unique characteristics, many of them were keen to know the difference between spicy Guatemalan coffees, full-bodied Javanese brews and sweeter Kenyan blends. And, once they'd decided on a drink, Starbucks would offer them a choice of flavoured milks and syrups to help them customise it. The approach seemed to work. By 1989, while sales of pre-ground coffee were still falling and the mainstream coffee industry was continuing to head down market, specialty coffee houses were taking 6 per cent of the market and sales of whole-bean coffee were growing at 30 per cent year on year.

That, it turned out, was only the beginning of a new relationship between Americans and their coffee. In 1989 there were only 585 coffee houses in the whole of the United States, but by 1995 there were five thousand; in 2003 that had leapt to 17,400 and by 2010 there were twenty-five thousand. As Starbucks and other big coffee chains grew into a corporate monolith and their stores began to look more like fast-food outlets than gourmet stores, some die-hard coffee enthusiasts have became disillusioned and drifted away. In a leaked company memo sent in February 2007, Howard Schultz complained of the 'watering-down of the Starbucks experience, and what some might call the commoditization of our brand'. None of that, however, should take away from its original achievement. Thanks largely to Starbucks, from the eighties onwards the mainstream coffee industry simply ceased to be the vehicle for good-quality coffee. In an otherwise declining business, the company helped turn what was in danger of becoming a generic commodity into a specialist one, one valued for its taste and not just its price. It did this not only by spending money on high-quality coffee beans and grinding equipment but by making coffee into an experience to be savoured in the company of others. Together with its fellow specialist roasters, Starbucks understood that fine coffee is something that people could take an interest in, and that spending time with other enthusiasts might encourage them to cultivate that interest.

The big beasts would eventually wake up and smell Starbucks' better-tasting coffee, and not only in the coffee industry. In an advertising blitz in 2009, the US division of McDonald's launched its McCafé brand of speciality coffee to compete with Starbucks. The following year Burger King retaliated by announcing that it would henceforth be serving Starbucks coffee in its restaurants. None of this was very surprising. Since the turn of the century institutions of all kinds had been looking into ways of reaching out to smaller groups. Most of them, however, were thinking less about the make-up of their products than the make-up of their audience.

2

Target practice

The evolution of niche

On how the big beasts tried to pick us off one by one

The clothing giant Gap, as we saw in the prologue, is one retailer that confronted the crack-up of mainstream culture. Around the year 2000, when young people began exiting its stores in huge numbers, Gap realised that it could not continue to be all things to all people – that there was no such thing as the average consumer. In its mid-life crisis, the company darted this way and that, chasing first after fashionably fickle teenagers, then doubling back to try to make it up to its faithful middle-aged following, before finally, in 2002, collapsing in a heap on the middle ground. In its desperation to win over everyone, Gap had only reinforced its reputation as a label that no one was mad about.

It was what the company did next that would come to define it. It called in Paul Pressler. Pressler, a charismatic forty-six-year-old marketer with the polished looks of a TV presenter, arrived at Gap Inc's San Francisco headquarters in September 2002 to take up the role of CEO. He had no experience in clothing retail, but was known to be evangelical about the power of market research and a genius with numbers. Pressler had cut his marketing teeth at Kenner-Parker Toys, working on the Care Bears characters, before being head-hunted by the Walt Disney Company to run its theme parks in 1987. While at Disney, he had won a reputation for the meticulousness of his methods. Children lucky enough to be taken on a Disney cruise to the company's private island in the Bahamas, for example, expected to arrive on a sandy beach with perfect seashells. 'When kids dug into the sand,' Pressler told a journalist, 'they came up with handfuls of perfectly polished, unbroken seashells. We knew they would find these shells on the beach because we planted them there every week. You can bet every kid went home with a pocket full of shells.'

True to his reputation, on Pressler's arrival in San Francisco he began by commissioning some research. For the first time in the company's history, Pressler hired outside market research firms to understand its customers around the world; for the first time, too, he hired a major Madison Avenue advertising agency, Leo Burnett, to take a look at Gap's various brands and refine their position within the market. Over the following two years Pressler conducted a battery of surveys and focus groups in which 320,000 Gap customers were canvassed for their opinions on all kinds of things. He used the data to divide up Gap customers into groups by age and gender and tailor the company's advertising accordingly: Gap began to run different ad campaigns for men and women. That, however, was only for starters. Pressler used the answers to his pollsters' questions to break down Gap's customers according to their psychographic values: whether they were 'style-conscious', for example, or lovers of 'updated classics'. He even hired a chief algorithm officer to analyse all the data that came in. In May 2004 he split up a group of twenty senior Gap executives into three teams and ordered them to accompany him on a world tour, armed with cameras, in search of consumer insights. One evening, after wandering around London's Tate Britain in search of inspiration, a Gap executive spied a pub with a chalkboard outside advertising its nightly specials. He took a photo of it and Gap stores all over world ended up with chalkboards in their denim departments.

Pressler's big idea was to use the wealth of market research at his fingertips to sharpen the focus of the brands. When customers told researchers that they wanted a range of different fits for the clothes in Old Navy stores, for example, Pressler gave them what they wanted – the original style was rebranded as Perfect Fit, a new style called Easy Fit was aimed at slightly older customers, while Tiny Fit was for trendy teenagers. When Gap customers said they wanted to feel 'individual and unique and not wear a uniform', the company launched a 'How Do You Wear It?' ad campaign to encourage a more personal approach to style, and hired Sarah Jessica Parker from *Sex and the City* to front it.

It didn't always work out as planned. When customers walked in to the stores, Pressler admitted, 'they didn't ask our store associates for help creating their own look. Instead they all pointed to the Sarah Jessica Parker ad and all definitively said: "I want that."' The big idea to emerge from all Pressler's number-crunching, however, was that Gap's three main brands – Gap itself, Old Navy and Banana Republic – were difficult to distinguish from one another. 'Our consumer-insight research showed that the three brands were sitting on top of each other,' he said. 'You could find khaki pants in all three and our consumer told us price was the only differentiator. Today, there's a tremendous difference.' To remedy this, Old Navy stores were charged more explicitly with the task of reeling in younger shoppers with less money, while Banana Republic was to raise its prices and go after a slightly older crowd. Gap remained in the middle of the market, but would no longer have to appeal to just anyone. Instead, it would focus more intensely on shoppers between eighteen and thirty.

Pressler's solution was to train his sights more firmly on the audience. For each of Gap's brands, he was going to carve out a niche.

2

In the autumn of 1999, as American teenagers were deserting Gap's stores, I was about to make an exit of my own. Lazing around in an Oxford college common room, it was the unconventional job title that made me sit up straight. 'Futurologist or trend-spotter wanted for global intelligence think-tank. Prominent New York-based communications agency requires social scientist who's up to the minute with what's new and what's next. Excellent rates of pay.' In among the adverts for summer teaching jobs, this sort of thing stood out. So did the employer: it had been placed there by a company called Young & Rubicam, which a swift Google search disclosed was one of the biggest and most respected ad agencies in the world. There was, I felt, no harm in applying. And then everything happened very fast. One week I was teaching politics and sociology and researching a doctorate, the next I'd morphed into a cool-hunter, working on New York time to research think-pieces on how to generate buzz around a product, earnest treatises on everything from the future of government to the future of youth culture, eager little research notes on the market for pet accessories among single women in their thirties.

Social critics like Dwight MacDonald and Vance Packard had inveighed against the rise of the 'questionnaire sociologist' in the fifties, but their ranks had steadily swollen to include me. And not only me. Flush with dollars from the dotcom boom, most of the big advertising agencies were trawling for academics to make them look clever in the eyes of their clients – not only number-crunchers but scruffy sociologists like me, earnest cultural-studies types, sleek semioticians, even the odd literary theorist capable of bluffing his way in hip-hop. By the end of the nineties there were legions of us broken-down intellectuals ambling down Madison Avenue. We had become the hunter-gatherers of the business world, paid handsomely to track the whims of the elusive modern consumer.

But how to go about it? Much of the research and writing work could be done from my digs in Oxford. There were occasional ethnographic field trips to observe consumers in their natural habitat – the supermarket or the nightclub, mainly – but most of my time was spent trying to make sense of the endless reams of data that came in from around the world detailing how consumers felt, either from interviews with them or via the thousands of trend-scouts we paid to keep an eye on them on our behalf. Armed with all that information, we were doing exactly the kind of work that Paul Pressler had recommended to his fellow executives at Gap: hatching new ways to slice the audience into neat little sub-groups so that businesses could target them.

This notion had come a long way since Alfred Sloan had had the idea of segmenting the market for cars into a series of income bands. Sloan had started out with the cars themselves and tried to match them to the different means of car-buyers. As the ranks of professional people-watchers grew, however, slicing up the market became less about differentiating products and more about getting to know the audience in the hope of selling them more stuff. It was relatively easy to use demographic data – raw information about the population gleaned from the census or voter lists – to delineate an audience according to their age, their gender, their sexual preferences, their ethnicity and where they lived. Since women did most of the household shopping, they presented an obvious target for certain brands. In the sixties they were joined by teenagers, a strange and exotic new species chased by advertisers and marketers. Pepsi set the balling rolling in 1961, allying itself with youth with injunctions to 'Think Young' and to become part of the 'Pepsi generation': taglines created for it by the venerable Madison Avenue agency BBDO, and which helped it steal a march on its fustier rival Coca-Cola.

By the late sixties, however, social changes began to upset the statistical apple-cart. The reverberations of the counter-culture had given rise to a generation keen to distinguish itself from the mainstream, and to a new kind of politics in which people were happy to identify themselves as women, gay men or black people. It had also, however, made them more stubbornly resistant to attempts to define them by the questionnaire sociologists. By the seventies, questions were being asked about whether identifying groups with increasingly tortuous combinations of demographic attributes was really hitting the mark. 'Are Grace Slick and Tricia Nixon Cox the same person?' asked one New York ad man in the *Journal of Advertising* in 1973, wondering what the daughter of the President and the lead singer of a psychedelic rock band really had in common beyond being young, white, well-heeled and well-educated women. Much the same was soon being said of demographic categorisation of the working classes. Classifying people by their job and their income made sense when workers were organised in trade unions and identified themselves as part of the same homogeneous group. But as unions fell away in the course of the seventies and eighties, and workers became more experienced consumers, the old categories didn't seem so sure a guide as to how they were going to vote or spend their money.

By the time I started working for a Madison Avenue ad agency, the audience was a rapidly shifting target. The response of questionnaire sociologists had been to observe it even more closely, in the hope of discovering sub-species within it. In 1994 the consumer-trends firm Yankelovich identified gays and lesbians as 'a distinct, highly influential and well-identified' consumer group, and marketers everywhere piled in to see who could be the first to net the lucrative pink pound. Then there was the single female consumer who, according to the data we had amassed at Young & Rubicam, had a huge amount of money at her disposal and was delaying marriage and children so that she could find the time to spend it ('Single women say "so long" to Prince Charming' was the tagline on the press release that accompanied our report). To get a better bead on their targets, we trend-spotters turned, like Pressler, to psychographics. Here again, Pepsi was an inspiration: on closer inspection its famous 'Pepsi generation' ads in the sixties were aimed not only at young people but at those who identified with the vibrancy of the youth culture emerging at the time – those who simply *felt* young. Any inquiry into psychographics, however, involved the endless ticking of boxes. Long-winded questionnaires invited our respondents to agree or disagree, mildly or strongly, with bald statements such as 'I think that the world is becoming a smaller place', 'I care about the environment' and 'I like to keep my house very clean'. Their answers were put to good use. Launched in 1949 by Procter & Gamble, Tide grew to become the biggest-selling American laundry detergent and the quintessential one-size-fits-all, mass-market product. Around the turn of the century, however, it began a merciless chain of sub-division. First to arrive were Tide High Efficiency and Tide Mountain Spring in 1997; five years later there was Tide Clean Breeze. Tide with a Touch of Downy came in 2004, and the year later after that Tide Coldwater. In the same year Tide with Febreze Freshness was launched, and in 2006 came Tide Simple Pleasures. The Tide Pure Essentials range arrived in 2007 and, in August 2009, as the global economic recession continued to take its toll, Procter & Gamble launched its bargain brand, Tide Basic. You could choose from among Tide Fresh Scent, Tide Glacier Scent, Tide April Fresh, Tide Clean Breeze, Tide Soft Ocean Mist, Tide Spring & Renewal, Tide High Efficiency, Tide Mountain Spring, Tide Tropical Clean and Tide Meadows & Rain. In just over a decade, the different varieties of Tide had multiplied to fill a whole shelf on the average supermarket aisle. They were all almost exactly the same, of course, but that wasn't the point – each had been lovingly crafted to hit a psychographic target identified by the company's army of market researchers. In July 2004, P&G's

global marketing officer James Stengel was able to boast to *Business Week* magazine that among his popular household products, there was 'not one mass-market brand, whether it's Tide or Old Spice. Every one of our brands is targeted'.

The hottest way of carving up the audience at the turn of the millennium, however, was according to when it was born. It meant that we questionnaire sociologists could combine impressive-looking demographic data about generational cohorts with a plausible list of psychographic characteristics that we could ascribe to each. Old people who had grown up during the depression of the late twenties and who had come of age during the Second World War were branded as a stoic, noble, greatest generation. Little seemed to be known about those who came immediately after, and so they were filed away as a mysterious silent generation. Then there were the loud-as-you-like, young-at-heart Baby Boomers who grew up in the sixties and seventies, and in their trail slouched in the cynical slackers of Generation X. The most recent addition to the marketer's armoury at the millennium was teenagers and young people born between the mid-seventies and 1990, known variously as Echo Boomers, Generation Y or simply the Millennials. The sudden enthusiasm for pink mini-skirts and luminous hoodies among Gap and its retail competitors, for example, was the product of excited data that the new generation of teenagers were making 40 per cent more trips to the shopping mall than anyone else, that it had huge amounts of money at its disposal and that its numbers were due to soar in the coming decade. It was also because, wherever the Echo Boomers went, we cool-hunters traipsed after them to note what they wore, the programmes they watched on television, the sports they enjoyed, the music they liked and the nightclubs they frequented. Survey upon survey paid tribute to a generation variously defined as technically savvy, politically liberal and uniquely self-confident. The kids were not only all right, they were awe-inspiring in every respect, and if any of us ever found out anything bad about them we didn't bother to write it down. Cheerleading for the deep-pocketed Echo Boomers went far beyond the shopping mall. In 1998, as we saw in the last chapter, James Cameron's *Titanic* was one of the last great Hollywood productions to appeal to everyone in the audience, but excitement about the film would probably never have caught fire had it not been ignited by a posse of Leonardo DiCaprio-fancying teenage girls. Even before *Titanic*'s release, its American distributor had organised test screenings that showed that teenage girls loved it more than anyone else. As a consequence, trailers for the film depicted a story of young love, with heavy emphasis on the gamin DiCaprio. Nearly half of all women under twenty-five who saw the film at the cinema went back at least once. It was, according to one ad woman, 'a watershed event, proving that girl power is a force to be reckoned with'. In the course of the next decade, virtually all of the ten highest-grossing Hollywood films would be summertime blockbusters, including *Harry Potter*, *Pirates of the Caribbean*, *Spider-Man*, *Shrek* and their sequels, films carefully calibrated to be just violent or risqué enough to squeeze into the parental guidance classification (PG13 in the US), which meant that they could be seen by huge numbers of teenagers.

Something similar had already happened on television, where the need to sell ads had made programme-makers even keener to find out who exactly was sitting at home watching them. In the mid-eighties the people meter, a zippy new kind of audience measurement, arrived, making it much easier to find out.

It wasn't long before the information made its way back to the commissioners. In the fifties and sixties, programmes like *I Love Lucy* and *Bonanza* had been made to appeal to everyone, but by the nineties they had given way to shows such as *Friends*, whose characters were more precisely aimed at the young adults between eighteen and thirty-four that advertisers most wanted to reach. By the turn of the century whole cable channels were being created to target the younger, juicier cuts of the television audience. In the UK in 2001, for example, the BBC announced plans for a new channel called BBC3 and Channel 4 launched E4; both were shameless plays by the industry's big beasts for exactly the same audience of teenagers and young adults. It didn't always work. Even if an age group could be targeted with any accuracy, there was no guarantee that the right kind of people would tune in. In the same year, BBC's Radio 4 launched a jaunty-sounding programme aimed at children and young teenagers called *Go4It*. Eight years later, however, it was finally forced to admit defeat and pull the plug on the show. The problem was that *Go4It* had only ever found twenty thousand young people in its target audience; the average age of its 450,000 listeners was between fifty-two and fifty-five.

And then, all of a sudden, the wind seemed to change. In retrospect, it would be easy to blame everything that happened next on a twenty-three-year-old jazz-piano crooner. In February 2002 Norah Jones, the daughter of Ravi Shankar, had released a folksy debut album called *Come Away With Me*. The album won some admiring reviews but no one expected it to sell very well, and it duly chugged along at the bottom of the charts. As the year progressed, however, sales began to quicken. The album seemed to have become the unofficial mood music for coffee shops and bookstores frequented by a discerning older clientele. Despite a lack of publicity, it was obvious that Norah Jones had somehow acquired a devoted army of fans. When Jones was invited on to *Saturday Night Live* in December of that year it gained even more momentum and, not long after that, it seemed to have become the ubiquitous Christmas present. By February 2003, a full year after its release, *Come Away With Me* had ascended to No. 1 on the Billboard album chart, where it remained for three weeks. In the same month it took five Grammy awards, including pop album of the year. From an almost inaudible start, *Come Away With Me* had risen on a wave of word-of-mouth interest to become the surprise hit of 2003. It had sold an incredible six million copies – most of them, a little research revealed, to music lovers at least two decades older than the singer herself.

To an industry whose revenues had been falling away for the previous three years, *Come Away With Me* must have seemed like a sign from the gods. Just like Gap, the big beasts of American music had grown fat in the previous decade; album sales had doubled in the nineties, the fastest spurt of growth in the industry's history. Beginning in 2000, however, they began a year-on-year decline from which they have never recovered. Part of the industry's problem was that it had become obsessed with all things teenage-friendly – rap, hip-hop and teeny pop – at precisely the same time that teenagers had worked out how to get their music for free on illicit online filesharing sites. What it had failed to notice was that the huge cohort of 81 million Baby Boomers, which vastly outnumbered teenagers, had never stopped bulk-buying the music that it loved. Between 1994 and 2003, according to figures crunched by the Recording Industry Association of America, sales of music to Americans of forty-five and older had grown from 15.4 per cent to 26.6 per cent of music sales; sales to those forty and older also increased, from 7.9 per cent to 10 per cent of sales. During the same period, sales to fifteen- to nineteen-year-olds had dropped from 16.8 per cent to 11.4. It was the same story elsewhere. At the beginning of 2004, for example, statistics from the British Phonographic Industry showed that for the first time ever, Brits in their forties were buying more albums than teenagers. If only by default, middle-aged people had become the fastest-growing segment of the music-buying audience and the same record-company bean counters who had done so much to single out teenagers barely missed a beat. In music stores all over America, store-fronts were gently rearranged, with much greater attention paid to anything that could be shoehorned into the category of adult music. By November 2003 new albums from Barbra Streisand and the Eagles had made their way into the Top 10, and a bevy of artists over forty, including Bette Midler, Van Morrison, Michael McDonald and Simon and Garfunkel, held eleven of the top fifty coveted spots in the Billboard chart.

The elaborate manoeuvres that took place in the music industry after Norah Jones didn't mean that retailers had turned their back on the impressionable teenage audience. Instead, they added fuel to the growing suspicion that there was no longer any such thing as a general audience. From now on there would be different kinds of audience, and while it would be ideal to bring all of them home, it had be admitted that some of them were so different as to be mutually exclusive. Some record stations, for example, refused to play Norah Jones, arguing that music which appealed to a middle-aged audience was bound to turn off their younger listeners. Music shows, such as the UK's *Top of the Pops*, which had lost their ability to focus on any particular section of the audience, were left to wither and die.

The big beasts of the music industry were not the only ones to wake up to the potential of an ageing society. It began to be mooted among the future-gazers reading the runes of retail sales that, while keeping their beady eyes on trendy young hipsters, marketers had taken their eye off the real prize of well-heeled older people. To us cool-hunters and futurologists it was as if someone had given our crystal balls a good shake, making everything look topsy-turvy and upside-down. Bugger youth culture, went the new mantra: a generation that once promised to die before it got old was now living out a middle youth, and it was up to us to help them feel good about it. Only two years after I had been hired to write fevered reports into the temperature of global youth, I was working for ad agencies and think tanks in New York and London to find out who older people really were – separating them out into different generational cohorts, for example, to work out what each cohort wanted. Whole days flew by in a research haze of Steppenwolf songs, day spas, and Stannah Stairlifts. Given that the words 'grey market' and 'old' had already been identified as insulting, I, along with a bunch of quietly bewildered twentysomethings, chewed over what to call the new objects of our attention. 'Middlescents' was rejected as too twee, 'third agers' was too distinctively American, 'new agers' too naff. 'Coffin-dodgers', my provisional suggestion, was met with silence.

In an interview with the *Observer* newspaper in August 2002, one ad agency trend-spotter went as far as to imagine how Nike might rework its famous tagline to catch the imagination of an older generation. 'Clearly there was a positive response to the "Just Do It" slogan amongst the risk-oriented active 16–20 group,' he said, presenting the fruits of his extensive research into the target group. 'However, research amongst the much less active 30+ group for whom sport is an occasional activity and sports clothing is more a form of relaxed leisurewear indicates that "Just Do It" may leave the brand limited to a youth niche, which in today's demographic of older people may severely limit sales. As a result, we recommend that a much more inclusive slogan, reflective of the real relationship the older target audience has with sport, would be more appropriate. For instance: "Just Watch It".'

3

In 1996 the most wanted woman in America was an inconspicuous suburban mother who spent much of her week hovering around the school gates. In the past she had leaned towards the Republican Party, but by the time that President Bill Clinton came up for re-election in 1996 her vote was considered to be for grabs. Clinton would send campaign workers specifically to hand her fliers. Bob Dole would name-check her during his roll-call of 'real Americans with real problems' in the final presidential debate. By the end of the year she would make it on to the cover of *Time* magazine.

Soccer Mom was the invention of political pollsters and, at least until the end of the presidential election, there would be plenty of journalists and pollsters to accompany her on the school run. The man most responsible was a Democratic Party strategist called Mark Penn. Beginning in 1995, Penn had begun to read through one hundred thousand interviews with American voters. His plan was to separate them out into a range of different sub-species of voter, and then arrive at a profile for each. This idea of identifying voter groups had been around since the eighties, but the groups chosen for closer inspection – Reagan Democrat in the United States, Basildon Man in the UK – were picked largely according to their income or social class. When Penn analysed the data, however, what he found surprised him. The usual demographic categories of class, race and age didn't show up significant differences in support between the incumbent president Bill Clinton or the Republican candidate Bob Dole. There remained, however, one issue that still had the power to divide voters: the experience of having had children. Childless voters were more likely to lean toward Clinton, but married couples with children were much more critical of the president. What Penn had discovered, he believed, was a sharp difference in mindset between childless unmarried voters and those who were married with children. He set about exploiting it, by targeting married couples and especially married parents.

While Soccer Mom was being wooed by Mark Penn, British political strategists were stubbornly pursuing her first cousin, Worcester Woman. Worcester Woman had been dreamed up by Conservative Central Office policy wonks in a blind panic, fearing that they might lose her to the new-look Labour Party. Tony Blair had one eye on Worcester Woman too, but with the other he had begun flirting with her husband, Mondeo Man. Blair was particularly fond of Mondeo Man because he had thought him up; the idea had come to him one morning, he said, when he noticed a man carefully polishing his Ford Mondeo outside his home. Here was, Blair felt, just the kind of middle-aged, middle-income, middle-management homeowner Labour needed to wrest away from the Tories with appropriate policies on public services and law and order. Soccer Mom,

Worcester Woman and Mondeo Man all arrived on the political scene because, at roughly the same time that marketing demographers were delineating the voting population using demographic and psychographic data, something very similar was going on in the political system.

Faced with the fraying of their traditional bases of support, mainstream political parties had begun to turn much of their fire on small groups of floating voters – what they called 'new political cleavages' – in the hope that their support might prove decisive in close-run states or constituencies at election time. Political scientists had long assumed that parties which wanted to win would line up the preferences of the voting population and make a beeline for the median voter. By the nineties, however, the middle ground had begun to give way and the median voter crumbled into a soup of different voting types. Peter Mair, now a professor at the European University Institute in Florence, has been studying political parties for nearly thirty years, and is now one of their most distinguished scholars. The way he explains it, winning an election used to be akin to sprinting around the top of a hill: smart political parties would stop as soon as they encountered the median voter halfway around. In the last few decades, however, that hill vanished and was replaced by dozens of hillocks, all of which politicians needed to spend time running around if they wanted to be elected. 'At some point the median became impossible to locate,' Mair told me. 'The average voter no longer exists.'

If the average voter had disappeared from the political landscape, it was proving difficult to get to know the new arrivals. Everyone knew that Soccer Mom, for example, was some subset of the white, female, middle-class suburban population, but after that things were a little more blurred. Define Soccer Mom as married, educated, and middle-class and she made up between 4 and 5 per cent of the American voting population, but relax those restraints a little and she grew to nearer 12 per cent. Then there were those on the fringes – Latino Soccer Mom, African-American Soccer Mom, lesbian Soccer Mom – who the pollsters didn't seem to be interested in at all. 'It's too broad a term,' Margaret Conway, political science professor at the University of Florida, told the *Florida Times-Union*. 'It assumes that people of a certain age group with children of a certain age group will all share the same views. It's an oversimplification of concerns and values.' Just because some mothers held down jobs, lived in the suburbs and had sons who liked to play football, it did not follow that they all thought alike or could be persuaded to vote in the same way. It was noteworthy, too, that only rarely if ever did so-called Soccer Moms claim the term for themselves. They simply couldn't identify with it, and not a few of them were insulted by the implication that they should.

Much the same could be said about attempts by political strategists to slice up the electorate according to their ethnicity, gender, religion or sexuality. So keen were they to neatly segment voters that they all too easily reached for stereotypes. But that wasn't the only problem. Even if Soccer Mom could be nailed down in terms of her values and attitudes, that still might not be much help in predicting her voting behaviour. There was precious little evidence, for example, that Soccer Mom had made any difference to the outcome of that 1996 presidential election. Herb Weisberg and April Kelly, two political scientists at Ohio State University who put together a measure of Soccer Moms from exit poll data, found that while Clinton had won more votes than Dole among Soccer Moms, that in itself was not out of the ordinary. He had, for example, won by an even greater margin among married women in general. 'There was,' Weisberg and Kelly concluded, 'no additional significant effect for soccer moms as we operationalized them.'

For a few years after the 1996 election, Soccer Mom continued to be wheeled out by the national media. In October 1998 she royally defied her stereotype by punching a referee after a soccer game involving her nine-year-old son in Virginia. It was shortly after that that Soccer Mom was replaced by Security Mom, a conservative-leaning mother who worried about al-Qaeda as well as football shirts and was credited by some with helping George W. Bush to a second term in 2004. By that time, however, the patience of the big beasts with attempts to slice up their audiences into pretty little segments based on their attitudes was wearing thin. That was hardly surprising. It was not clear, for example, that isolating different generations from their environment and putting them under the microscope could tell us anything meaningful about what made them tick. In the early nineties demographers had appropriated the idea of Generation X to brand all of us born between the mid-sixties and late-seventies as work-shy slackers. Our apparent hostility to the work ethic, however, had less to do with our attitudes than the fact that the majority of us came of age at a time when good jobs were perilously difficult to find. When the economy picked up in the late nineties and many of my peers proved themselves to be productive and entrepreneurial, the whole idea of a lackadaisical Generation X had to be abandoned.

It wasn't only the demographers and the political strategists who were getting cold feet. When the Economist Intelligence Unit surveyed two hundred senior corporate executives in

2004, 59 per cent reported that they had paid for a major segmentation exercise of this kind during the previous two years. Only 14 per cent, however, said that the segments arrived at were useful for anything. Perhaps as a result, questionnaire-carrying cool-hunters were being elbowed aside in favour of more high-tech weaponry. By raiding huge vaults of data about our shopping habits from credit-card companies and retailers, and then adding that to what they already knew about us, pollsters could separate us out more accurately into different species of consumer. More important, it could actually help them get a sense of what we might do next. The big beasts had started out dissecting us according to how much we earned, where we lived, what age and gender we were and what sexual partners we preferred. When we moved around too much and the accuracy of those classifications was called into question they added further data on how they presumed we felt. When even that proved an unreliable indicator of which way we might jump, they moved on to track us through our patterns of consumption. In practice that meant peering into our shopping bags and even our fridges – trying to trap us, like wild animals, according to what we ate.

This kind of thing is no longer very difficult to do. For some years now, huge data-mining companies have been selling on data about our buying habits sourced from credit-card companies. The American firm Claritas, for example, collates conventional demographic data about where we live and what age we are with information about our shopping patterns to produce a system called PRIZM, which can separate us out into different clusters. In 2009 it counted sixty-seven different varieties of American, including 'movers & shakers', 'money & brains', 'young & rustic' and 'urban achievers'. The beauty of systems like PRIZM lies in their ability to home in on us street by street or house by house, making more traditional ways of targeting an audience look clumsy. PRIZM's British equivalent is Mosaic, which classifies the entire British population into similar clusters based largely on purchasing data drawn from its owner, the data giant Experian. Mosaic updates its system twice a year. In September 2009 it redrew its clusters using a total of 440 different variables drawn from 21 billion bits of data to divide us up into 155 kinds of person, 67 household types and 15 social categories including 'claimant cultures', 'suburban mindsets' and 'industrial heritage'.

Among political strategists, these methods have come to be known as 'micro-targeting'. Micro-targeting was pioneered by George W. Bush's chief strategist, Matthew Dowd, in the wake of the 2000 presidential election. Dowd and his colleagues decided that the Republican Party needed to win by a more convincing margin in 2004 so, under the supervision of Karl Rove, Bush's leading guru, they began to look into the kind of cluster analysis developed by data-mining companies. Just like the cluster analysts, they started out with conventional demographic data and then mixed in information from the data-mining companies about our shopping patterns. They then polled a sample of the population and used all the data at their disposal to predict how similar people would have answered the same questions. In doing so, they were able to separate out Americans into thirty-four different sets of like-minded people – groups like 'downscale union independents', 'tax and terrorism moderates' and 'older suburban news-hounds' – and predict which issues they would be interested in and how they would likely vote. Having identified groups of Republican-friendly voters, they could then set about tailoring messages for each. If the poll suggested that Latino American men in their thirties with children, who subscribed to the *New Yorker*, didn't always vote but, if they did, were predisposed to vote for Bush, micro-targeters could make a note for someone to call them early on election day to remind them to go to the polling station.

The growing popularity of micro-targeting means that while we voters choose politicians in the ballot box, those politicians are quietly choosing us too. Since 2005, the three major British political parties of Labour, Conservative and Liberal Democrat have been using Mosaic to embark on their own exercises in micro-targeting. To their practitioners, these exercises have all the precision of a natural science: Alex Gage, one of Bush's 2004 campaign team, has compared the process to identifying a strain of DNA. Micro-targeting has also changed the reasons why politicians might want to target voters in the first place. Whereas Bill Clinton had set his sights on small groups of hazily defined swing voters like Soccer Moms, Dowd's team attempted something much more ambitious: to identify citizens who might be persuaded to vote Republican based on what they were eating, drinking and buying. The telescopic accuracy of the data has done something else, too. It has made political geography much less important. Pollsters used to focus their efforts on districts where they had a reasonable political presence; now they could use much more precise tools to ferret out small pockets of Republican-friendly voters in Democrat areas. By adding in data about people's preferred foods, the size of their mortgages, their hobbies and the places they liked to go on holiday, they could also move beyond traditional ways of targeting voters – by their neighbourhood or their ethnic origins – to zero in on people as individuals. The data Matthew Dowd was able to marshal in 2004 suggested that Dr Pepper was a Republican drink, whereas Pepsi was a firmly Democratic beverage. Gin and vodka were Democrat, whereas Republicans favoured bourbon and red wine. Similarly, as he told the *New York Times*, 'anything organic or more Whole Foods-y skews more Democratic'.

The problem is, many of us have begun to eat very different things. Think about what happened to Mondeo Man. When Tony Blair conjured him out of thin air in the mid-nineties he was – albeit in a primitive, scattergun way – trying to identify a new kind of voter according to the car he had chosen to drive. Almost as soon as he did, however, sales of the Ford Mondeo began to fall off a cliff, plunging almost every year from 127,144 in 1994, according to economists at IHS Global Insight, to a mere 44,150 in 2008. Our tastes are prone to change over time, which makes them an unreliable indicator of who we are. Perhaps because of our resistance to being defined in this way, many of us have also learned to stomach a wider range of things at the same time. John Goldthorpe, a sociologist at Nuffield College in Oxford, has been keeping a wily eye on delicate changes in the structure of British society for some decades. In 2004, together with his colleague Tak Wing Chan, Goldthorpe was allowed a look at the full set of data from a recent government survey into the musical tastes of the English. What they found was that the relationship between social class and cultural consumption in England was no longer very clear – that there was no longer a firm distinction between moneyed, educated classes with the time and inclination for highbrow music such as opera on the one hand and the pop-loving masses on the other. In place of traditional cultural snobbery, however, was a whole new kind of showing-off. What distinguished those at the higher end of the social spectrum was that their cultural diet was wider in its range: 'comprising,' according to Goldthorpe and Chan, 'not only more "highbrow" culture but in fact more "middlebrow" and more "lowbrow" culture as well'. The best way to think about it, they continued, was that as people got richer and smarter they were morphing from 'univores' interested only in consuming one kind of music into 'omnivores' who were quite happy to dip in and out of different musical hierarchies. Arguably, our growing omnivorousness goes far beyond our taste in music. It may well help us explain why, in just a few decades, football terraces that were once populated almost exclusively by white working-class men are now frequented by a much broader range of the population. But it may not be as innocent as it looks. In fact, according to the sociologists, it is quite possible that this omnivorous new audience might signify a new kind of cultural one-upmanship, that it is 'no less directed towards the demonstration of cultural and social superiority – that is, when set against the very restricted cultural styles of univores'.

The appearance of a new breed of omnivore who knows how to pick and mix its cultural diet from ever more exotic and extreme combinations is one more reason why middlebrow, mainstream culture has found itself in trouble. One of the defining features of middlebrow culture was that it presented us with a ready-made selection box from which we could choose. As such, it presents an obvious headache for the hunter-gatherers charged with tracking us via the food that we eat. The weapons invented to pick off audiences have evolved in the last half-century from a blunderbuss into a high-velocity sniper rifle. Even then, however, they are liable to fall wide of their target. Just because I watch football on Saturday afternoons doesn't mean I won't head to the opera in the evening. Just because you usually buy your food from the supermarket's own brand doesn't mean you're not going to try something from the premium range tomorrow. And, whatever Matthew Dowd says, it doesn't follow that just because someone shops at Whole Foods they are going to dash out and vote Democrat. Far from it. In 2006, the American journalist Rod Dreher argued the existence of a new type of Birkenstock-wearing, nature-loving, granola-munching Republican, the Crunch Conservatives.

*

What became of that big-game hunter Paul Pressler? For the first couple of years his strategy of separating out the audience for each of Gap's brands into different age-groups seemed to be faring rather well. In the spring of 2004, after a hike in sales, he was being touted by New York's stock market analysts as a miracle worker. By autumn of that year, however, the recovery had stalled and sales at all three Gap brands began to head south.

Pressler's response was to go back to the numbers, to recalibrate each brand to focus even more closely on its segment of the population. Not only that, but judging that Gap was still failing to persuade women over thirty-five back into its stores – the company was only taking 3 per cent of that market, as opposed to 8 per cent of the under-thirty-fives – he made plans for a new range. To get inside the heads of his target customers, Pressler commissioned yet more research. Gap's ethnographic researchers visited women between thirty-five and forty-five in their natural habitat, peeked inside their wardrobes and followed them around on shopping trips. The upshot was an entirely new brand, Forth & Towne, a name that had been chosen to evoke a friendly meeting place. 'Forth' was doubly significant as this was, after all, to be Gap's fourth main brand. By the summer of 2005 it was ready to be unveiled, and so in August Pressler invited an influential group of analysts and financial bigwigs to join him at one of the biggest shopping malls in America, the huge Palisades Center in West Nyack, New York, to show them around the first ever Forth & Towne store.

In his welcome address Pressler talked up his 'multiple-pronged approach' for growing Gap's business. The idea of Forth & Towne, he told his audience, 'really began with identifying a need in the marketplace and an opportunity within our portfolio. Gap, as you know, holds either the number one or the number two specialty market share for segments under the age of thirty-five, using age as a proxy for our customer base. But we don't yet have a significant share of the segment over thirty-five. So targeting this group is really the next natural step for us to expand on our portfolio.' When he had finished, Pressler invited Austyn Zung, the design chief of Forth & Towne, to deliver a tribute to the wisdom of the older woman. 'I believe women of this age are very savvy,' she told her audience. 'They know exactly what they want. This customer is stylish. She is grown up, and she is elegant.' She knew this because of her extensive research. 'We have great insight into our customer. It has helped us understand her and how each brand can best serve her.' Zung proceeded to outline her plans to chop up the over-thirty-fives into four different types – Allegory, Vocabulary, Gap Classic and Prize – each of whom would get their own range of clothes. Prize woman, for example, was the sort whose 'wardrobe is based upon clean simple comfortable silhouettes. Our jersey dressing gives her the comfort and simplicity that she is looking for as a wardrobe builder.

She complements these basics with decorative elements such as printed blouses and tunics and bold chunky jewellery. Her free spirit and sense of adventure show in her style. I think of this woman as a traveller who is inspired by far-off places, different cultures and people even only if in her mind.'

The audience of hard-headed analysts did not seem overly impressed. When the time came for questions, one wanted to know why, if Gap thought the over-thirty-fives were such a distinctive market, it was choosing to associate its name with Forth & Towne. When Paul Pressler announced that Forth & Towne would stock sizes all the way from 2 to 20, on the basis that 'one thing we learned in going out and talking to this customer and shopping along with her, they come in many different shapes and sizes', another rather pointedly asked whether Gap was trying to cater for the older woman or the larger one: 'My question is about whether your commitment is to the older woman or the larger woman. And it seems like you are trying to do both. And I'm wondering how that works. Does the size 2 shopper want to shop where the size 20 shopper is?' Both of them had a point. American women over thirty-five might have told researchers that they wanted special treatment, but it didn't follow that they wanted to be lumped together with all other women their own age. In fact, they may have wanted just the opposite. 'The truth is,' the New York marketing consultant Mary Lou Quinlan told the *Washington Post*, 'Baby Boomers do not see themselves in their chronological age. They always see themselves as younger.'

In trying to decant its customers into neat little containers, Gap was always in danger of both patronising those whom it included and alienating those who were left out. What was revolutionary about Frank Winfield Woolworth's approach to retailing at the end of the nineteenth century, as we saw in the last chapter, was that he charged all his customers the same fixed price and treated them all the same. But big beasts like Gap were implicitly admitting that some of their customers were more valuable than others. The inevitable consequence of this was to further demoralise what was left in the middle. By slicing away all those different age groups and feeding them to Banana Republic, Old Navy and now Forth & Towne, Pressler had cannibalised Gap's core brand. It is not only the big beasts of retail who have stumbled into this trap. When broadcasters pare off sections of the audience for niche digital channels, for example, they often leave the programming on their flagship channels looking pallid and generic. And when politicians spend much of their energy homing in on small sections of the voting population, they risk further alienating the rest of the electorate.

In retrospect it might have been better if Paul Pressler had listened to the audience assembled in front of him in that New York mall instead of the audience he and his hunter-gatherers had put together with their flip charts. When, in 2006, the company hired the rapper Common to hype Gap's new range of hoodies with a ditty known as 'Holiday in the Hood', it only sowed more confusion about what the brand stood for. By the beginning of 2007, after sales in its stores had declined for twenty-eight of the previous thirty-one months, Pressler handed in his resignation. A few months later Gap closed all nineteen of its Forth & Towne outlets and, not long after that, it ceded its title of the world's biggest clothing retailer to the Spanish firm Zara. The company's last advertising campaign before Pressler's departure was called 'Fall into the Gap'. The tagline was apt, because that was exactly what had happened to the company. For several decades Gap had succeeded in building a bridge across the middle of the market, in being all things to all people. Around the year 2000, however, that bridge began to crumble and its customers began to flee. They've been fleeing ever since – between 2004 and 2009, the company's total sales fell 11 per cent, from $16.3 billion to $14.5 billion. In an unfamiliar retail environment, Gap had responded by taking pot-shots at the parts of its audience that it thought it could identify on the basis of their age. But instead of filling in the holes which had appeared in the mainstream, that only made them worse, and many of its wares fell straight through the gap.

3

The Mole

Burrowing under the mainstream

In which the big beasts try to live underground

In 2004, while Oxford sociologists were mulling the significance of a growing number of cultural omnivores in the audience, I was taking a crash-course in how to be one of them. On a rainy Sunday in September, while everyone else sat at home in their slippers, I was among twenty-five thousand people huddled under umbrellas in Trafalgar Square listening to the Pet Shop Boys perform a brand-new soundtrack to the silent, black-and-white film *The Battleship Potemkin.* When it first made an appearance in 1925, Sergei Eisenstein's reconstruction of a naval revolt was a masterpiece of avant-garde film-making and a thrilling homage to the newly minted Bolshevik revolution. Now, thanks to London's Institute of Contemporary Arts (ICA), it was playing on a giant screen in London's tourist ground zero while an electro-pop duo stood around listlessly adding tinny synthesisers and bassy boop-de-boops to its scenes of mass demonstrations and Cossack brutality. A montage of images from Trafalgar Square's history as a gathering point for political protest was played to lend the event added significance, and a 26-piece German orchestra, the Dresdner Sinfoniker, sat on the side of the main stage to add a little cultural heft. Mel Brooks was in the audience, possibly scouting for new ideas.

At first glance, the ICA sits in enemy territory. Since 1968 it has been resident on the Mall, London's most imperious thoroughfare, sandwiched between Trafalgar Square and Admiralty Arch at one end and Buckingham Palace on the other. Across the way is Horse Guards Parade, where the Queen steps out to inspect her cavalry, and just beyond that lie Whitehall and the whole machinery of British government. In a listed, white-stucco fortress of a building which had once been one of the capital's most sought-after residential addresses, on a street frequently plumped up with Union Jacks and the sound of marching bands, the ICA has for more than sixty years been charged with bringing radical culture to British audiences. It is easier said than done.

Avant-garde was borrowed from a French military metaphor, and it originally referred to the advance guard of an army pushing into enemy territory. In its heyday in the first few decades of the twentieth century, to be avant-garde meant having the derring-do required to open up pathways through difficult or unknown cultural terrain so that everyone else could follow. A commitment to the avant-garde meant having little respect for either tradition or audience; it required an overwhelming break with the traditional way of doing things, and often came with radical ideas about transforming society too. It also involved smoking out its enemies. When mainstream, middlebrow culture arrived in the twenties and thirties to feed a general public which had grown hungry for culture, it wasn't long before the two were at loggerheads. Middlebrow presented itself as a culturally enriching menu aimed at the general reader, viewer and listener, and defined itself as in direct opposition to the highbrow and the avant-garde – the sort of culture that, felt the mandarins of middlebrow, too easily led to self-referential gibberish which deliberately excluded those who weren't in the know. Enthusiasts for high culture and the avant-garde were quick to return the favour. In an unpublished letter to the *New Statesman*, the unashamedly highbrow Virginia Woolf dismissed middlebrow culture as 'betwixt and between ... neither art itself nor life itself, but both mixed indistinguishably, and rather nastily, with money, fame, power, or prestige'. In 1960 Dwight MacDonald, the same critic who had spoken out against the methods of the questionnaire sociologists, used an influential essay called 'MassCult and MidCult' to denounce middlebrow's mixed up, watered down, vulgarised reflection of the living culture of the avant-garde. 'A tepid ooze of midcult is spreading everywhere,' he warned, and was in danger of infecting everything that it touched. The only solution for the avant-garde was, he implied, to fall back to a defence of their own camp.

As mainstream culture continued to grow, that lofty approach began to look less attractive. By the seventies it was more or less as dead as a dodo. Anyone with avant-garde sympathies who wanted an audience for their work needed somehow to engage with the kind of mainstream culture that people saw on their televisions and newspapers without entirely surrendering to it. One way to outdo the mainstream was to mix up different cultural brows, genres, disciplines and boundaries with much more shameless gusto than it could ever do.

Hadn't even fusty old Dwight MacDonald, in his 1960 essay, paid tribute to the promiscuous *joie de vivre* of the kind of culture which delights in 'breaking down the old barriers of class, tradition, and taste, dissolving all cultural distinctions. It mixes, scrambles everything together, producing what might be called homogenized culture, the homogenization process that distributes the globules of cream evenly throughout the milk instead of allowing them to float separately on top.' By the turn of the new millennium a new breed of omnivore had arrived in the audience who liked to try very different things. The result was that ostentatious cultural mix-ups were all the rage, and that Pet Shop Boys/Eisenstein/Dresdner Sinfoniker crossover was a perfect example of the breed. Even if some of them looked better on paper than they did up close, the passing visitor could hardly fail to be impressed by their stirring ambition. By then, however, I was more than a passing visitor. The man whose hard work had brought that whole Trafalgar Square extravaganza together, the ICA's director Philip Dodd, had just hired me as his portentously titled Director of Talks. Dodd was an academic whom the lure of the zeitgeist, together with the ICA's always-precarious finances, had transformed into a relentless cultural fixer. He would glide around its musty corridors like an apparition, throwing off cultural combinations from behind a long black overcoat that stuck to him like a cloak. To veteran staffers, he was known as Count Doddula.

Thus far, this book has been about the problems faced by big beasts who have, for most of their lives, enjoyed something close to a monopoly over mainstream culture. But the slow crack-up of mainstream culture didn't only affect them. It was also of serious concern to places like the ICA that defined themselves against mainstream culture; as much as the big beasts, they were still working out how to adapt to their new environment. By the time I started work there it was obvious that the relationship between the mainstream and those who had set themselves against it had become hopelessly compromised. An open-air screening of revolutionary propaganda in London's most illustrious public square might once have been a coup perpetrated by mischievous activists, but now the *Battleship Potemkin* performance came courtesy of London's mayor and the generous patronage of a major management consultancy firm. Afterwards, the ICA threw open its stunning regency-era rooms for a lavish after-party to show that it could mix people as well as culture. The then Mayor of London, 'Red Ken' Livingstone, swapped stories with pop stars; strutting West London writers danced the night away with newspaper columnists; countless cultural intermediaries mingled on the balconies and had themselves a well-deserved smoke. To add to the air of bacchanalian camp, a crew of waiters wearing sailor suits mingled among the guests and served a generous supply of beer and vodka from the Russian drinks company that was sponsoring the event.

2

If standing aloof from mainstream culture with the dwindling remains of the avant-garde was no longer an option, and sitting on the sidelines mixing things up like a cultural DJ didn't always work, a more reliable alternative was always available to the ICA: to look underground. The avant-garde, after all, was not the only current running against the tide of mainstream culture. Since the sixties it had been joined by a new breed of cultural troublemaker – youth subcultures, veterans of the counter-culture and a new generation of anti-capitalists – all of whom were hostile to mainstream culture and the big beasts who peddled it. Beneath the surface was soon a teeming, rambunctious underground populated by different varieties of cultural mole who were determined to burrow under its authority. It was as if each of them had decided to wage a new kind of subterranean war against the mainstream, popping up to poke fun at its pieties and generally doing their best to shake it out of its complacency. The ICA, in search of fresh impetus and new audiences, was more than happy to make common cause with them. In 1976, amid mounting social unrest and the outbreak of punk, it was hosting some of the first underground gigs by The Clash. Born out of an underground scene in New York, London and Sydney, by the sweaty summer of 1976 punk had given rise to a shock-haired, safety-pinned new subculture whose anarchic get-up and music had the authorities seriously worried about the moral fibre of the young. In the same year an ICA exhibition called *Prostitution* featured images of a performance artist called Cosey Fanni Tutti from her work as a porn model. The result precipitated a flood of hate mail, and so scandalised mainstream culture that the ICA was paid a visit by officers from Scotland Yard's Obscene Publications Squad.

The appearance of subcultures like punk excited the interest of academic sociologists. In his 1979 book *Subculture: The Meaning of Style*, the British sociologist Dick Hebdige went as far as to imply that punk, with its 'radical aesthetic practices', was a worthy successor to avant-garde movements such as Dada and the Surrealists. Far more important than what these subcultures shared with the avant-garde, however, was what they had in common with each another. Punk, after all, wasn't the only underground movement to appear in the course of the sixties and seventies. There were hippies, mods, rockers and casuals too, and before long youth culture was buoyed up by a shifting array of tribes, each with its own distinctive dress codes and rituals. What united them was that they existed firmly under the radar of mainstream culture and defined themselves against it with gestures of defiance or contempt. Skinheads shaved their heads to give the finger to mainstream society; hippies ingested LSD to escape it; mods mounted gleaming Italian Vespas to outrun it; casuals sported high-end designer gear to outclass it. None of this activity on the margins could have taken place, Stuart Hall pointed out in his book *Resistance Through Rituals*, except as a reaction to the steady growth and expansion of mainstream culture itself – the rise of mass consumption, a huge expansion of higher education, the formidable influence of broadcast media and a consensus that brought together the major political parties – which seemed to those in the underground to be gathering up everyone it could into suffocating, anonymous drudgery.

It wasn't very long before it was trying to gobble up the tribes of youth culture too. Here, after all, was a free laboratory to which they could look for inspiration and new ideas. For those of the underground, the prospect of selling out promised a decent return on their talents. In 1991, when a post-punk band from Seattle's grunge scene sold their second album, *Nevermind*, to the record industry titan Geffen (Nirvana's first had been released by the independent label Sub Pop), and it went on to sell ten million copies, the guerrilla war between subcultures and the big beasts of the mainstream seemed to have settled into an uneasy, but mutually rewarding, truce.

Traffic between the mainstream and the margins continued at a lightning pace. As the conveyor belt ferrying morsels from the counter-culture and alternative subcultures into the mainstream speeded up, it was often difficult to tell who owned what. With its quirky flavours and unapologetic activism, the Vermont ice-cream company Ben & Jerry's has long been seen as an icon of anti-capitalist cool. When, in April 2000, its hippy founders Ben Cohen and Jerry Greenfield announced that they had sold their entire operation to the multinational food giant Unilever it seemed as if the last leftovers of the counter-culture had been scooped up and swallowed whole. (The founders of Innocent Drinks, a more-holistic-than-thou British smoothie company, would follow their lead in April 2010 by selling off a majority stake to Coca-Cola.)

No sooner had subterranean tunnels been dug than the big beasts would show up and try to inveigle their way in. One result was the appearance of a new kind of intermediary whose job it was to shine a light into the cultural undergrowth and bring back titbits that might be of interest. For example, by playing Nirvana's 'Smells like Teen Spirit' endlessly throughout the autumn of 1991 the teen-friendly music video channel MTV was almost single-handedly responsible for catapulting the band into the cultural mainstream. The traffic also went the other way. In June of the following year, when MTV did Bill Clinton the favour of introducing him to its sought-after youth audience during his bid for the presidency, his appearance marked the beginning of a new age in which politicians would realise that it was no longer possible speak to everyone at the same time. In a way, we cool-hunters, trend-spotters and future-gazers had become intermediaries too. The whole point of cool-hunting was to spend time undercover in youth subcultures (some aficionados called it 'deep hanging out') and bring back insights that might find their way into the mainstream –

the time frame for movement between the two, I was informed by one of my futurological employers, was between twelve to eighteen months. Stealing the techniques of the underground could be just as rewarding as borrowing their street cred, and many of the best insights could be gleaned from anti-capitalist activists. The Vancouver-based anti-advertising magazine *Adbusters*, for example, is run by an audience of activist media workers jaded by the advertising industry; its artwork is designed to flip the meaning of advertising campaigns and thereby shock audiences out of their consumer delirium. Highlights have included a vodka bottle embossed with 'Absolut Nonsense' and a spoof on a Tommy Hilfiger campaign featuring a herd of sheep and the tag line 'Tommy follow the Herd'. At the same time, their colleagues in the Culture Jammers Network – the paramilitary wing of the movement – are hard at work using guerrilla tactics to play companies at their own marketing game: subverting brand messages at street level, parodying advertisements, altering billboards and placing satirical advertisements.

By the year 2000, however, both had begun to encounter a problem: mainstream advertisers were paying people like me to reach into their creative armoury and help themselves. Baulking at the phenomenal expense and clutter of the mainstream media, the big beasts had realised that a good way to manufacture buzz or a tipping point for their products was to shock their audiences with frightening, offensive or taboo images. Another was to use street-level stunts, which became known as guerrilla marketing. The upshot was a phoney war between mainstream brands and anti-branding activists in which it was often difficult to tell the difference between them. A subculture of street-level activists, a Bronx-based graffiti gang called the TATS Cru, even shuffled off en masse to create street advertising for companies such as Coca-Cola. It was partly my fault. During my years working for advertising and marketing agencies I spent a good deal of my time researching strategies for buzz and guerrilla marketing, and much of my inspiration came from the other side. I wasn't the only one; to this day I've never encountered an advertising executive who didn't have a well-thumbed copy of Naomi Klein's *No Logo* on their bookshelf. It wasn't only the activists that we stole from. In 2002, while I was in the pay of a trend-spotting consultancy called HeadlightVision, the *Sunday Times* revealed that the company was advising big companies to add 'criminal kudos' to their brands in the hope of buying them some underground cool. One client, a brand manager for Hula Hoops, rather sheepishly informed the reporter that while the research was very useful for spotting new techniques in guerrilla marketing, 'we are not doing anything particularly relating to gangsters. We are selling a packet of crisps at the end of the day, and there is only so much you can do with it.'

Trend-spotters weren't the only kind of intermediaries to increase their influence around the turn of the century. By the time I arrived at the ICA, it had become a kind of cultural intermediary. Whereas Dwight MacDonald had complained that middlebrow culture was stealing avant-garde wares and passing them off as their own, the ICA was now quite happy to be thought of as a kind of culture-gazing futurologist, going deep underground to bring advance notice of new culture, ideas and trends that would reliably show up in the mainstream later on. For the most part, we were very good at it.

Lately, however, the blurring of the line between the cultural margins and the mainstream had been confusing us too. Perhaps that was why my first attempt to scandalise the mainstream could not be judged an unqualified success. A month after the Pet

Shop Boys spectacle, myself and my colleague Jennifer Thatcher put together a series of debates, films and performances called ErotICA, which wondered whether there was any difference between pornography and stripping and the burgeoning appetite for high-end erotica among the chattering classes. We set about inviting strippers, burlesque performers and the odd cultural commentator to a festival of events. Given the ICA's reputation for investigating the relationship between porn, exploitation and art – the Cosey Fanni Tutti episode, for example – our intention was to mix things up a bit and ask some interesting questions. If we were honest, though, it was also to attract some rhetorical outrage and free publicity from the mainstream media. To some extent, it worked. 'Porn at the ICA splits art world', screamed the headline in the *Sunday Times* the weekend before the events began, before listing a lurid line-up of 'striptease artists from a burlesque ensemble called the Whoopee Club and a performer called Mr Teds, a half-pig/half-woman character who dances on ice skates wearing only tassels'. In the same article, an ICA spokesman was quoted as saying that 'the idea is to give a voice to an underground experience which is creeping through London'.

Our insistence on the underground nature of our work, however, was a little rhetorical. If burlesque was sweeping through the city it wasn't very far underground. It was simply a bunch of nice arty girls taking their clothes off (bar the tassels) and having a good time. Then there was the strangely muted reaction to the show. Despite the best efforts of the *Sunday Times*, there was no furore in the art world or anywhere else about what we were up to with ErotICA; the only hitch occurred when our star guest, a Derrida-reading Parisian porn star called Ovidie, pulled out in favour of a more lucrative gig. There was hardly anyone left to be shocked, mainly because the big beasts of mainstream culture had long ago borrowed shock tactics from the cultural underground and were using them in everything from public health advertisements to fashion campaigns. As a ploy used by subversives to terrorise the mainstream, shock was not only dead but festering. The most galling verdict on EroticICA came from *The Economist*. Their reporter had called up one of my old colleagues from HeadlightVision, who concluded that audiences were now bored with sexually explicit advertising messages. They were, apparently, on the lookout for something more subtle.

3

In some ways, this muddying of the water between the cultural margins and the mainstream was only to be expected. Mainstream culture hasn't been around for very long. Its growth can be traced to the middle decades of the twentieth century, when the big beasts of mainstream culture began to serve up pre-digested slices of culture to a general public that had become newly hungry for it. By the seventies, since much of the fresh talent and ideas was hiding out underground, it made perfect sense for them to want to feed on it too. As the traffic between margins and mainstream quickened it was if the big beasts were engaged in a game of Whack-A-Mole, bringing their mallet down on a succession of plastic moles just as soon as they popped their heads through the holes on the board. Among alternative types this game is often the cue for a weary discussion of the voracious appetite of mainstream culture, its ability to devour almost anything and turn it to its own advantage. But that doesn't tell the whole story. Since the nineties, there has been a curious shift in the predatory habits of the big beasts in relation to their prey underground. When Geffen signed Nirvana in 1991 they didn't do so because they wanted to water down their music and serve it up in a more digestible form. What they wanted was for the band to remain at a distance from the mainstream; after Nirvana, most alternative or indie music took its place apart from mainstream culture in a genre of its own. When Unilever bought up Ben & Jerry's, they didn't do so to make it more like Unilever, and after 2000 Ben Cohen and Jerry Greenfield sounded like the same hippy activists they always had been. No longer did the big beasts want to digest underground culture and absorb it into the cultural mainstream. Instead they preferred it to stay where it was – underground.

The Nirvana and Ben & Jerry's of the film industry was Quentin Tarantino, a former video store worker turned independent film-maker. Between Sergei Eisenstein's *Battleship Potemkin* and the films of Quentin Tarantino, film-making outside the commercial mainstream had come a long way. By the seventies so-called indie cinema had come to mean the kind of edgy, taboo, intimate, quirky, subversive and often subtitled films which were anathema to Hollywood, and which were put together on low budgets outside the studio system. Indie films played to loyal but tiny art-house audiences such as those at the ICA, or at annual jamborees like the Sundance Festival, an offbeat showcase for American independent cinema inaugurated by Robert Redford in 1978. Held deep in Mormon Utah, Sundance was well out of the way of anyone who didn't really want to be there, and it quickly established itself as America's most crucial testing ground for independent cinema and a mecca for ambitious film-makers. It arrived at just the right time. While they ruthlessly zeroed in on the teenage audience in the eighties and nineties with 'event' films and their sequels, the big beasts neglected those moviegoers who were looking for higher-quality fare. For the first decade of its life, Hollywood's big beasts took little notice of the films which were shown at Sundance. In 1992, however, a tall, geeky director arrived in Utah to show his first film – a gruesomely ironic, low-budget twist on the heist genre called *Reservoir Dogs*. *Reservoir Dogs* was enough to make Tarantino the talk of Sundance but, just like every other film on show at that year's festival, it didn't escape its indie niche to find a mainstream audience.

It was, however, enough to get him noticed by the bearded, legendarily bullish film impresario Harvey Weinstein. In interviews Weinstein likes to claim that his love affair with art-house cinema stemmed from an incident in his youth when he paid to see Truffaut's film *The 400 Blows* in the mistaken belief that it was a porn film. In 1979 he set up a small independent film studio called Miramax and, together with his brother Bob, begun distributing modestly budgeted, intelligently made films like *The Crying Game* and *Sex, Lies and Videotape*. By the early nineties he had acquired a reputation as a marketing genius, possessed of a rare alchemical ability to turn obscure indie films into 'breakout' or 'crossover' successes. His wizardry often involved tinkering with the films themselves, which was how he acquired the nickname Harvey Scissorhands. When, fresh from Sundance, Quentin Tarantino arrived in Weinstein's Hollywood screening room to show him *Reservoir Dogs*, Harvey didn't much like the look of it. Specifically, he hated the film's gruesome torture scene in which a psychopathic bank robber uses a razor to sever a policeman's ear. In an interview with Peter Biskind for his book *Down and Dirty Pictures*, Tarantino recalled some of the frosty exchange that followed:

Weinstein: Without this scene, you have a mainstream movie. With this scene you put it in a box. Without that scene, I could open this movie in three hundred theatres. As opposed to one! Thirty seconds would change the movie in the American marketplace.
Tarantino: Harvey, no. I think the movie is perfect the way it is. I think the torture scene – it does put the film in a smaller niche – but I think it's one of the best things in the movie.
Weinstein: Well, okay, then, and I want you to remember it was Miramax that let your movie go out exactly the way you wanted it!

In retrospect, Quentin Tarantino believes, this conversation was the pivot on which everything else turned, and that by wrestling it his way he was able to force the direction of his entire career. Unfortunately, the same could be said for Harvey Weinstein. *Reservoir Dogs* itself did not cross over into mainstream cinemas – it took no more than a million dollars at the American box office – but its successor made up for it. At a cost of only $8 million, *Pulp Fiction* went on to make $100 million for Weinstein and Miramax in 1994, and the canter of movie executives making their way to Utah turned into a unruly stampede. After *Pulp Fiction*, both Sundance and Harvey Weinstein became too important for Hollywood's big beasts to ignore. Just like the ICA or the New York cool-hunters, Sundance became a cultural intermediary, ferrying films as well as talent from indie cinema out into the open, where they could be snapped up by Miramax. By then, the company was in the pay of one of Hollywood's big beasts; in search of the funds to make films like *Pulp Fiction* as well as to distribute them, the

Weinstein brothers had sold Miramax to the Walt Disney Company in 1993. 'We've taken films out of the art house ghetto and brought quirky new sensibilities to mass America', a triumphant Harvey Weinstein told *Time* magazine in 1997, in an attempt to explain why he had just been named in its list of the twenty-five most influential Americans alive. He was not wrong. In that same year Miramax came away with twelve Oscars – more than any studio had won since 1939, when MGM took eight just for *Gone with the Wind*.

It was shortly after his appearance in *Time* that things began to turn bad for Harvey Weinstein and Miramax. The problem was not difficult to identify. Just about every major Hollywood studio had, in the course of the nineties, decided that it wanted an art-house division of its own and had bought up a small independent studio for the purpose, and so Miramax's carefully cultivated point of differentiation no longer meant very much. But there was another, deeper problem with Weinstein's strategy. Since the late eighties Miramax had succeeded in bringing indie films to big audiences through judicious marketing and sheer bull-headed hard work. Puffed up with the prestige of *Pulp Fiction* and bolstered by Disney money, however, the budgets for Miramax films began to rocket. Not only that but Harvey Scissorhands was still hard at work in the cutting room, insisting on changes to make his films more palatable to mainstream audiences. As the decade drew to a close, the result was that beneath their art-house veneer Miramax films looked very much like mainstream fare: lavish historical romances like *The English Patient*, tepid costume dramas like *Mansfield Park*, flimsy romantic comedies like *Shakespeare in Love* and kitsch like *Captain Corelli's Mandolin*. At around the same time Harvey Weinstein's eye began to wander, and he spent less time on art-house cinema and more on empire-building – turning Miramax into a publisher, launching a magazine, making the company look indistinguishable from big media beasts such as Fox or Paramount. The big beasts, meanwhile, did exactly the opposite. In the last decade they have cleverly deployed indie as a marketing tool, discreetly making indie films via their boutique labels and then pushing them out to court high-end audiences. Many of these films began to deliberately mimic the tropes and stylistic tics of indie cinema – alienated teenagers, dysfunctional families, meditations on suburban soulnessness, self-consciously quirky humour and a generous resort to shock tactics or the taboo – in a shameless play for the indie crowd. 'There's now a great deal of confusion out there over the notion of independent cinema,' the film writer David Thomson told me. 'It was once an attitude to the medium, but now it's just a stylistic distinction, a pose.'

As much Nirvana's post-punk indie music, independent cinema has quietly become a genre of its own under the protection of the big beasts. The formula seems to work. By 2006, releases from indie studios earned a total of $1.2 billion at the American box office, accounting for 12 per cent of all movie revenues. In that year, the biggest splash at Sundance was made by *Little Miss Sunshine*, the tale of one family's desperate road-trip to be present at a beauty pageant where their seven-year-old daughter has been chosen to participate. The following year it was the turn of *Juno*, a quirky coming-of-age pregnancy film with a jaunty soundtrack. Both films wore their indie credentials on their sleeves when they were released, despite the fact that they were owned and distributed by Fox Searchlight, the boutique, independent arm of Twentieth Century Fox. Miramax was still capable of pulling in Oscars, but it had drifted away from its indie bolthole just at the time when the big beasts decided that it was one worth moving into. The company, which had set out to outfox the big beasts, found itself outfoxed by them. In 2005, after one too many costly flops like *Cold Mountain* and bust-ups with Disney, Harvey and Bob Weinstein left Miramax to set up their own independent production company, The Weinstein Company, where they have struggled to retain their touch ever since.

At least some of Hollywood's new-found interest in indie cinema can be attributed to the kind of target practice whose rise was traced in the last chapter. Just as the big beasts of the music industry woke up to middle-aged audiences after the success of Norah Jones, the big beasts of Hollywood have in the last decade warmed to the kind of quality films that might appeal to an older crowed. There were good reasons why they should. After a decade of decline, the average age of cinema-goers has been creeping upward since the late nineties, partly because teenagers had taken to watching DVDs or playing video games at home. Throughout the nineties young people between the ages of fifteen and twenty-four made up by far the biggest chunk of the British film-going audience, but by 2006 they had been outnumbered by the over-thirty-fours. To make their foyers appear more grown-up, many cinemas added in-house coffee shops and patisseries.

It can hardly be a coincidence, too, that in recent years a wave of low-budget, low-audience indie-like pictures have swept the boards at the Oscars. The five biggest films at the American box office in 2008 – *The Dark Knight*, *Iron Man*, *Indiana Jones and the Kingdom of the Crystal Skull*, *Hancock* and *WALL-E* – were mostly aimed at teenagers. There was no overlap whatsoever with the five films vying for the Best Picture Oscar in the same year. *The Curious Case of Benjamin Button*, *Frost/Nixon*, *Milk*, *The Reader* and *Slumdog Millionaire* all looked very much like indie films, even though many had been financed and distributed by the big beasts of Hollywood. When Steven Spielberg came to make *Jaws* he drew upon the counter-cultural paranoia that had pervaded the work of Martin Scorsese but dragged it from its art-house ghetto into the mainstream. What was happening now was just the reverse. The big beasts were buying up indie studios not to invite them into the mainstream but to keep them in a self-consciously indie kennel outside. The result has been the triumph of a kind of film that, at best, will be seen by about 10 per cent of the cinema-going public. Quality films made for everyone have given way to quality films made very consciously for a high-end, grown-up niche.

It was not just older moviegoers who had sparked the interest of Hollywood's big beasts in independent cinema. For the big beasts, one of the best things about indie films – apart from the fact that they are cheap to make – was that its fans actively wanted to be together in the same audience. The problem with slicing up people into different demographic groups, we saw in the last chapter, is that they had a nasty habit of wriggling out of their pigeon holes. Indie audiences were different. Just like the cultural underground from which they came, they were thick with cultish clumps of fans who identified both with each other and against the mainstream audience – and who could be relied upon to tip each other off about which films were coming up. As the control of the big beasts over their audiences loosened they began to pay more attention to these small groups of tightly knit, reliably loyal audiences. It was not only art-house audiences who whetted their appetite; there were plenty more underground players where they came from. Keeping its ear to the cultural ground, for example, the ICA had long tried to attract an alternative crowd by targeting the same kind of demographic characteristics favoured by the big beasts – black musicians, for example, or gay writers, or women film-makers. At one point we even organised a Welsh night. More popular than any of them, however, were zombies. By the time I arrived at the ICA horror films had become a thriving subculture, brimming with enthusiastic fans who were all passionate advocates for the genre. Then there were sci-fi buffs, graphic novel aficionados and technology geeks, all arranged in their own tightly defined and carefully cultivated fields. The ICA invited them all in, and before long it was infested with a teeming population of subcultures. These new arrivals didn't have the rebellious swagger of earlier movements like punk, but just like them they often came with dress codes and rituals, and took great pains to define themselves as apart from the mainstream. Nor is it only the ICA which is being eaten away at by the growing population of moles. With the success of series like *Lost*, *True Blood* and *Heroes*, quality television is now richly populated with vampires and superheroes that draw on the enthusiasm for their cultish popularity. When David O. Selznick wanted to assemble an advance audience for *Gone with the Wind*, we saw, he organised a press conference and announced a nationwide talent search for his Scarlett O'Hara. When James Cameron was ready to show a teaser for his long-awaited 3D film *Avatar* in July 2009 – an epic freighted with the same blockbusting ambition of its predecessor *Titanic* – the first place he went to rustle up an audience was at Comic-Con, the annual get-together of comic-book, fantasy and action-adventure fans. An auditorium of six thousand geeks hung on his every word.

Audiences like these buy books in huge numbers. Mainstream

fiction is usually identified with the kind of middlebrow, realist novels that take their drama from the stuff of everyday life, the sort of literature that could rely on getting reviewed on the books pages of newspapers, on being talked about on highbrow television and on taking pride of place at the front of many bookshops.

The gatekeepers of the literary mainstream have traditionally turned their noses up at genre fiction, which they consider to be rote and formulaic rehearsals of familiar storylines. In turn, many fans of genre fiction are prickly and resentful at their exclusion from the mainstream, which only reinforces their idea of themselves as an underground club. But while the mainstream literary canon has been spreading itself thin to shore up flagging sales, genre literature has been getting smarter and attracting some distinguished recruits. The Booker prize-winning and formidably erudite former literary editor of the *Irish Times* John Banville, for example, now writes detective novels under the *nom de plume* of Benjamin Black, and has won some highly enthusiastic reviews for his work. This new kind of genre writing has also attracted the attention of the big beasts of the publishing industry, and it is not hard to see why. Writers are drawn to it because they hold the key to larger audiences of devoted fans; marketers like it because it lends itself well to sequels; and bookshops like it because they know where to put it in the shop. The upshot is that the audience for books is shifting from the middle to the margins. The book-loving general reader, whom the big publishing beasts did so much to court in the middle decades of the twentieth century, is losing ground to a different breed of book-buyer: someone who owes their allegiance not to books in general but to a passionate attachment to a particular genre.

*

In the early nineties the comedian Bill Hicks used to begin one of his skits by suggesting that everyone in the audience who worked in advertising or marketing should immediately kill themselves. The problem, he went on, was that any marketers or advertisers in the audience would likely be giggling along and nodding their heads in agreement. They would all be sitting there, he quipped, quietly congratulating him for having the good sense to court the lucrative anti-marketing demographic. Hicks, who made a career out of throwing stones at mainstream America, was ahead of his time. For forty years the moles of underground culture have defined themselves against mainstream culture and the big beasts that controlled it. With the caving-in of middlebrow culture, however, the relationship between moles underground and the big beasts above them has become more complicated.

When the old hierarchical walls that separated the different cultural brows collapsed, it seemed as if everything would be ceaselessly mixed up with everything else. It didn't happen. Audiences have certainly become more culturally omnivorous, but they could easily mix up cultural ingredients on their own and didn't need anyone else to do it for them. No matter how hard institutions like the ICA tried to stir different kinds of culture together, they separated out again. And when they did, something else became clear. Instead of being mixed up together, each of them had settled into its own place in a new cultural environment. In this new cultural ecosystem, the relationship between the margins and the mainstream had been twisted out of all recognition, and the only thing that mattered was to lay claim to an identifiable niche. As their control over their audience loosened, the big beasts began to look underground in search of some reliable mouths to feed. For their part, the moles of the counter-culture and subculture continued to burrow away and seek each other out. But if the moles imagined that they were eating away at mainstream culture, they often did so blindly oblivious to the fact that it had already caved in above them, and that its big beasts had been forced to adapt in order to survive in a hostile new habitat. The big beasts are now targeting them rather than the other way around, and their custom has become just another niche in the market.

They would soon have company; the internet makes it much easier for people to seek each other and form a subculture apart from the mainstream. But even before that happened there was one more unexpected result of this shifting relationship between the big beasts and the underground. The traditional passage from underground to the mainstream, the time that had to be served scratching around on the margins before being ushered into the mainstream, did not really exist in the way that it once had done. To survive and prosper in this new cultural ecosystem, one needed to focus on carving out a distinctive niche and growing a fertile and engaged audience around it. At the ICA we found this out a little too late. In 2005 Philip Dodd left and a likeable journalist called Ekow Eshun was appointed as the ICA's artistic director. Once again, it was no easy task. Partly because we had been colonised by lots of very different subcultures, it was felt that the public no longer had a clear idea what the ICA was, and Eshun was charged with bringing the place to their attention. To do that, he decided, we needed to take the plunge and go a little more mainstream – 'to talk to as wide an audience as possible', as he put it. The plan was to entice people into the building with a few middle-of-the-road crowd-pleasers and then stun them with the kind of recherché stuff that we really wanted them to see.

To implement it, Eshun hired a management team largely made up of people whose previous jobs had been in the mainstream media. The first thing to go was our logo. In 2006, a design agency was hired to change the ICA's austere, staunchly modernist logo to something a little more inviting. When their handiwork was unveiled later that year the three letters of the acronym had been replaced by a bunch of differently sized bubbles and the full 'The Institute of Contemporary Arts'. The bubbles were supposed to represent water molecules; when they were animated, the idea was that they would move around to suggest the dynamism and diversity of everything the ICA does. The staff were sceptical but everyone else seemed delighted. In interviews to announce the relaunch, the creative director of the design agency responsible told journalists that his intention was to make the ICA look less dry and more welcoming. 'The use of its full title, The Institute of Contemporary Arts, is quite deliberate,' he explained to *Creative Review*. 'It marks a move away from being just for those "in the know" and reminds people why they should visit.' It wasn't just our logo that merited a fresh lick of paint. We paid questionnaire sociologists to roam around the building and find out what our audience wanted. The next time the ICA came to mount a spectacle in Trafalgar Square, in 2007, Eisenstein and the avant-garde had been ditched in favour of a live show by the Chemical Brothers, a band that had emerged from the mid-nineties underground club culture, but who now looked decidedly middle of the road. In return for a dollop of sponsorship we mounted an exhibition of snaps taken by artists and celebrities on their mobile phones. We played host to REM and dedicated an entire exhibition to photographs of the band. We invited Paul McCartney into the building to play a live set, even though by then he wasn't at the cutting edge of anything but divorce law.

There were other wheezes too, but none of them worked. Plenty of people turned up to see the Chemical Brothers, REM and Paul McCartney, but they weren't really interested in the ICA and they didn't hang around long enough to try any of our home-grown, spicier fare. By the end of 2008 everyone had to admit that in launching ourselves into the mainstream we had fallen flat on our face. Not only had we sowed further confusion about what the ICA stood for, we had also annoyed what remained of our core following. In 2009 the management team departed as quickly as they'd arrived. Soon after that our bubbly new logo was airbrushed out of existence – an urgent staff memo arrived in the email telling us to 'please avoid using the logo with the bubbles wherever possible' – and we reverted to the plain old ICA. Like many fringe or marginal operators before it, the ICA had arrived at the point at which it was happy to 'sell out' to mainstream culture, but no one wanted to buy it.

4

The Hawk

Cutting through the foliage

In which the prey becomes predator

On 1 April 2009 a teenage boy from Oxford was swapping messages on Facebook with a girl three thousand miles away in Maryland when he announced his intention to kill himself. 'I'm going to do something I've been planning for a while,' he typed, 'then everyone will find out.' In Britain, the time was half past eleven at night. The girl from Maryland knew next to nothing about the boy from Oxford; they were friends only on Facebook and had never met. All the same, she decided to tell her mother. Taking the threat seriously, her mother picked up the phone and called her local police station. The Maryland police officers put in a call to a special agent working at the White House, who in turn phoned the Metropolitan Police in London. At 12.26 a.m. on Thursday 2 April, less than an hour after the electronic suicide note had been sent, the Met alerted the operators at Thames Valley Police's Oxfordshire control room.

It was at this point that the high-speed transatlantic chase arrived in the in-tray of Paul Sexton. Sexton was acting police inspector for Oxfordshire that night; eight months later I met him in an Oxford restaurant littered with Christmas decorations to find out what happened. Even puffed out by his policeman's bullet-proof vest, Sexton is small and slightly built; he is also relentlessly chipper, possessed of the ability to take control of any situation and try to find a way through. I'd arrived at the wrong place for our rendezvous, but Sexton duly appeared in a mammoth police van, instructed me to get in the back and whisked me away to his favourite place to eat. When news of the suicide threat was phoned in from London, he told me, he wasn't at all sure what to make of it. The message had been sent on April Fool's Day, and for all he knew it could have been an elaborate hoax. Even if it was real, it gave him and his officers little to go on. The only information the boy had divulged on Facebook was his surname and what seemed to be the name of an Oxfordshire school, which is why the case had ended up on his desk. It might have been possible to go through the usual channels and extract more information from the girl's computer or from Facebook; but that would have taken far too long and, as Sexton says, 'time was ticking'. Instead, he and ten of his colleagues knew instinctively what to do: they set about Googling him.

'We were just playing with the name, playing with the school,' says Sexton. 'It helped that the surname was a little out of the ordinary. What we were looking for, both on Google and the online version of the electoral register, were families of that name who lived near the school that we were pretty sure the boy attended. It was a game of trial and error.' According to detailed police notes made at the time, it took Sexton and his officers just ten minutes to get four possible leads for the boy's location; by 1.42 a.m., after a little more Googling, they had narrowed it down to eight possible addresses in Oxford and a couple in the outlying areas. 'At that point we thought – enough, let's go door-knocking.' Sexton sent two carloads of officers around to visit each of the addresses, raise the occupants from their beds and explain their morbid race against time. At the fifth of those addresses, a home on the outskirts of Oxford, they finally got lucky. There was no answer at the house itself, but a next-door neighbour told the two police officers that a teenage boy lived there and that he was a student at the school they were looking for. Sexton had just authorised his officers to break the door down when the parents appeared blearily at the door. Accompanied by the police officers, they went to their son's room and discovered him barely conscious after a potentially lethal cocktail of sleeping pills and alcohol. The boy was rushed to hospital, where he made a full recovery. The police officers had arrived at 2.49 a.m., a little more than three hours after the boy had typed out his electronic suicide note, and just in the nick of time. 'The euphoria when the news went out on the police radio was just unbelievable,' recalls Paul Sexton. At 3.31 a.m. he asked one of his control-room operators to phone the woman in Maryland and tell both her and her daughter the good news. The notes record her relief and exhilaration. 'Two continents pulled together,' she said, 'and managed to save a life.'

The international rescue played out between Maryland and Oxford that night was nail-biting stuff, but it was only a dramatic example of a game of online hide-and-seek that we play every day. Over the last decade we've become voracious consumers of electronic information. Google started out with a mission to organise all the information on the web and make it available on its search engine; flush with its success, it began turning everything else into electronic information and making that searchable too. If the company has its way, we'll soon be able to browse through the entire history of human literature and download it on to our desktop computers.

The result has been to make us into what the philosopher Daniel Dennett and the cognitive scientist Steven Pinker call informavores: creatures whose natural habitat is online, and who exhibit an almost unlimited appetite for the information we find there. The novelty of scavenging through all that information, however, is wearing off. With an almost unlimited menu at our fingertips, many of us have become highly skilled at using search engines to get exactly where we want to go.

Sitting alone in his bedroom, that suicidal boy was able to bypass the usual institutions of school, church and neighbourhood and seek out a direct connection with a girl thousands of miles away. Since Paul Sexton's police officers discovered evidence of the boy's interest in illicit suicide websites in the week prior to his attempt, it is even possible that a shared interest in the subject is what brought the two together in the first place. But that wasn't the only way in which the net changed things. In spending time online the boy unwittingly left an electronic trail of clues to his identity and, to make sense of those clues and get to him quickly, the police officers needed to narrow their field of attention too. To do so, they cut through the usual channels of police enquiry and put their faith in Google.

As we spend more time with electronic information, we are becoming just as impatient. In 2004, according to a survey by the web expert Jakob Nielsen, 40 per cent of us visited a website's homepage and then drilled down to where they wanted to go; four years later, that figure had fallen to 25 per cent. We are learning to go straight to what we want. Between 2007 and 2009, according to another study, the number of searches in the United States involving just one word decreased from 24.5 per cent to 20.4; during the same period the number of searches encompassing three or more words grew to become the majority. More than just informavores, we're evolving into ruthless information predators.

Our hawkish approach to online information is fast finishing off what remains of mainstream culture. Even before we began to spend much time online the mainstream was floundering and in poor shape. The big beasts who had traditionally controlled it enjoyed a monopoly over our attention as we sat in the cinema or shopped on the high street, and used it to feed us a pick 'n' mix selection of ingredients they had chosen for us. As we slipped away from their grasp in the last few decades, many of them spread themselves ever thinner in an effort to reel us back in, but that only made their mainstream, middlebrow fare look samey and indistinguishable. They also trained their sights on the audience in the hope of picking off its juiciest parts, but their attempts at target practice often fell wide of the mark. Then came the internet. Even more than the shopping malls and out-of-town supermarkets that lured custom away from high-street stores, vast virtual supermarkets like Google, iTunes, Facebook, eBay and Amazon have cultivated whole ecosystems that work by inviting just about everything on to their turf. When everything is tagged with electronic information and set free in a virtual ecosystem, the pick 'n' mix looks even less appetising. Not only can we graze at our leisure, but they allow us to become information predators, slicing through the cyberspace undergrowth to locate exactly what we're looking for. With this incredible bounty to choose from, anything that gets in our way tends to be left for dead. From prey at the mercy of the big beasts, we have become their predators.

2

How did people seek out things that were hard to find before the internet? Often they tried leafing through the small ads. Printed text advertisements are almost as old as the printing press itself. The first to be printed in Britain, a statement of rules for how the clergy should celebrate Easter, was printed up in 1477 by the same William Caxton who had introduced the printing press to Britain the year before. As printed matter evolved into magazines and newspapers, along came the classified ad – lists of pithy little text ads, classified according to type and studied carefully by job-seekers or anyone who was looking for somewhere to live. It wasn't long before they were being used to search out other people too. By the beginning of the twentieth century, H. G. Cocks writes in his book *Classified: The Secret History of the Personal Column*, the small ads were home to a thriving underground world of correspondence columns, lonely-hearts clubs and shady matrimonial bureaux. They had also become a haven for subcultures – gay men and women as well as swingers or sexual adventurers – who were shunned by polite society. Spirited euphemisms began to abound: gay men took to identifying themselves as 'musical', 'unconventional' or 'artistic', while women who called themselves 'sporty' usually did so to indicate they were lesbian. Just in case the penny still hadn't dropped, many ads mentioned an enthusiasm for the works of Oscar Wilde.

Newspapers and magazines were the perfect place for the small ads because they had an exclusive hold on our attention for the time we set aside to read them. In advertising terms, a newspaper is simply a package or bundle of things rolled up together to attract the attention of the audience that flicks through it. At first, that was not very difficult. Printing presses are expensive, and those who owned them enjoyed a collective monopoly over the news and information they served up. They used it to feed us the news and information that they felt we needed to know. The diet began to grow. As the masses became hungry for news and newspaper barons realised that they could sell their assembled audience on to advertisers, newspapers became valued middlemen and extended their remit beyond politics and business into the stuff of everyday life – crime and sport, for example. The way that newspapers covered politics and business changed too; to the simple chronicles of what had happened they added colour, context and what later became known as human interest. As much as Woolworth's stores, Penguin's paperbacks or Hollywood's films, newspapers had by the middle decades of the twentieth century evolved into pillars of middlebrow culture.

For a long time, it worked. Between 1932 and 1957, according to Francis Williams in his book *Dangerous Estate: The Anatomy of Newspapers*, national daily newspapers in Britain had increased their readership by 90 per cent, and thirty million newspapers were making their way into British homes. But if anything, Williams notes, the number of titles was dwindling. For the most part, those that remained were owned by a few wealthy families, and the iron grip that they had on their audiences meant that they became licences to print money as well as stories. They also kept getting bigger; it was during these boom years, Leonard

Downie, Jr. and Michael Schudson point out in an article in the *Columbia Journalism Review*, that newspapers began to cultivate 'a much broader understanding of public life that included not just events, but also patterns and trends, and not just in politics, but also in science, medicine, business, sports, education, religion, culture, and entertainment'. As newspapers expanded both their size and their readership, they brought within their pages everything from lowbrow TV listings to highbrow arts criticism. Dedicated book supplements, for example, appeared to guide the general reader through the task of selecting a book. The *Washington Post Book World* started life in the sixties, while the *Los Angeles Times Book Review* came along in 1975. Along with the *New York Times Book Review*, they soon became essential accompaniments to the menu of middlebrow literature. Most of the expansion was supported by advertisers: as the classifieds were joined by bigger, glossier ads that took up whole pages, newspapers became one of the most powerful forms of advertising ever invented. 'You name it,' says James Twitchell, author of *AdCult USA*. 'The appearance of ads throughout the pages, the "jump" or continuation of a story from page to page, the rise of sectionalization (as with news, cartoons, sports, financial, living, real estate), common page size, halftone images, process engraving, the use of black-and-white photography, then color, sweepstakes, and finally discounted subscriptions were all forced on publishers by advertisers hoping to find target audiences.'

In the eighties and early nineties, however, large publicly owned conglomerates bought up many family-run newspapers. To recoup the vast sums of money they had spent, and to squeeze out a little extra for their shareholders, they began to fire journalists and buy in column inches from news agencies. The change, says the journalist Nick Davies in his book *Flat Earth*

News, was most visible at local level. Between 1986 and 2000 over half of the journalists on British local papers lost their jobs; in a single year, 1996, a third of those local newspapers were sold to new owners. Just as Woolworths and high-street book chains tried to trim their costs by centralising their buying, the effect was to shift decision making from locally based editors to faceless corporate boards and diminish the individual papers' ability to supply readers with the genuinely local news stories that they wanted to read. This cost-cutting was most ferocious in the United States, particularly among the large regional papers and general-interest magazines which had the firmest grip on their audiences. Even before the internet arrived to loosen their hold over the flow of information, many American papers and magazines had been squeezed half to death by their owners. At the same time, they kept expanding their remit, gobbling up new areas of interest and muscling into the public conversation about everything from reality TV to the Royal Family in order to hold the attention of their audience.

Throughout the nineties newspapers put on a huge amount of weight, but much of the extra bulk consisted of little more than advertising vehicles hitched clumsily to a flagging editorial engine in a desperate effort to deliver eyeballs to advertisers. The cracks began to show. Straining themselves to cover the whole beach-front, general-interest papers and magazines often ended up diluting their authority and their reputation for quality. Since the zenith of its popularity in the late seventies the circulation of *Reader's Digest* in the United States had nosedived from seventeen million to below eight million. When it responded by trying to feed those readers a generic diet of celebrity stories and household tips that they could easily find elsewhere, yet more were driven away. In August 2009 *Reader's*

Digest filed for an embarrassing bankruptcy, and in February 2010 its British subsidiary followed suit. The lavish books supplements inside newspapers also began to shrink or even disappear, and the few that survived often sacrificed depth for breadth. In 2009, when the *Washington Post* followed the *LA Times* by shutting its stand-alone books supplement, it seemed to herald the end of an era of salaried critical authority and a final nail in the coffin of mid-list, middlebrow bookselling.

Newsrooms, meanwhile, saw the growth of a kind of journalism that has little time for cultivating contacts and researching stories, churning out recycled, rarely checked stories that can be put together with the help of a news service, a press release or Google. A report published by the Project for Excellence in Journalism in February 2009 revealed that the mainstream American media is now so stretched that big stories are sometimes not covered at all. In the same year, a study of the five most prestigious general-interest papers in Britain – *The Times*, *Guardian*, *Independent*, *Daily Telegraph* and *Daily Mail* – found that 60 per cent of their output consisted wholly or mainly of news-service stories or press releases, while a further 20 per cent of the stories were slightly adapted from the same. Since they were relying on much the same raw material, newspapers had become fatter at the same time as their unique output was becoming thinner. Like the mainstream coffee industry they had plumped up their product with filler – inferior quality, generic news instead of original reporting. As much as Woolworths or General Motors, the stuff they offered us began to look pretty much the same.

After years of these painful cuts, newspapers and general-interest magazines have been forced to take the plunge into a vast ocean of online information. On the internet there is an almost limitless supply of news-like information, most of it available for free. In this vast new information ecosystem, newspapers have finally been forced to surrender their monopoly on our attention. In February 2009, according to the researchers at Harvard University, the average American internet user spent sixty-one hours and twelve minutes online in a month, but only 1.2 per cent of that time – forty-three minutes and nine seconds – was spent looking at newspaper websites. Newspapers thrived when they were able to exert a hypnotic hold over a captive audience, but with so much free information to choose from the spell is now wearing off. In most developed countries, newspaper circulation and the advertising that went with it are in long-term retreat. Twenty out of thirty OECD countries are witnessing a decline in the circulation of their newspapers, according to a study published in 2010 by the OECD itself: sales of American papers had plummeted 30 per cent in the previous three years, it discovered, while those of British papers had dropped 25 per cent in the same period. The irony is that news itself is flourishing and being read by more people than ever – just not in papers.

What is novel is the way we hawkish information predators pick our newspapers apart online. So quickly can we zoom in from anywhere in the world that we're learning to scavenge our news from a wider range of sources, using search engines, links or recommendations from friends, and we spend less time with each paper. In September 2009 the websites of seven of Britain's biggest national papers recorded an amazing 153.2 million visitors, only 35.7 per cent of whom came from the UK. But how are they being read? In June of the same year, while the print version of the *New York Times* was being read by 1.6 million people and holding their attention for half an hour each day, the paper's website had 17.4 million visitors from around the world; each of them, however, spent an average of just fourteen minutes and twenty-nine seconds there in the whole month. 'Although the readership of newspaper websites grew rapidly,' complained Downie and Schudson in their *Columbia Journalism Review* article, 'much of the growth turned out to be illusory – just momentary and occasional visits from people drawn to the sites through links from the rapidly growing number of web aggregators, search engines, and blogs'. It is not that we have given up on news, in other words, it's just that we're consuming it differently, ripping through online newspapers to find exactly what we want. For newspapers, this presents yet another problem. Just like many general-interest retailers and manufacturers, many of them have spread themselves too thinly trying to do too many things. Now they'd like to put a value on their product and charge us for it, but the news they're producing doesn't seem very different from the abundance of information available for free – indeed, it might even have been culled from there in the first place.

Even worse for newspapers, we are applying much the same hawkish logic when it comes to seeking out other people. The news industry cleverly positioned itself between those who had something to sell and those who were looking for something. It used to be that if you wanted to look for a job or a flatmate, the only way to do it was to buy your local paper and read through the small ads. Seeking out the things that we're looking for, however, has become much less onerous since the early days of the classified section. No-frills online classifieds sites such as Craigslist and Gumtree work by inviting everyone on to their patch and letting them search around and find each other for free. In such information ecosystems buyers and sellers no longer need chaperones like newspapers to introduce them. The number of Americans who use classified ads websites such as Craigslist, according to a survey from the Pew Internet Project, more than doubled between 2005 and 2009; a tenth of the population now uses them on a daily basis.

Craigslist was invented by an internet entrepreneur called Craig Newmark in San Francisco in 1995, and now operates classifieds sites in more than five hundred cities around the world. By March 2009 it was the most often searched-for keyword on American search engines, with more traffic than eBay or Amazon. Newmark calls himself the Forrest Gump of the internet; on his page on the Twitter messaging service he talks as much about the problems encountered by his garden bird-feeder as he does about Craigslist. When I caught up with him in a San Francisco coffee bar he seemed almost embarrassed by his achievement. 'I'm only a nerd,' he said, by way of introduction.

Each Craigslist site is home to a vast jumble of advertisements in various categories, but since all are tagged with online keywords they're also fully searchable, which means users can locate exactly what they want much more quickly than they could by leafing through the classified ads. 'Craigslist is simply a way for people to get everyday stuff done and to help each other do it,' Newmark told me. 'I mean stuff like getting housing, a place to live or a job, buying and selling your stuff. Those are all very mundane things, but it's how you get through the day. It's basically people finding each other by searching.' With this formula, Craigslist and sites like it did much to hasten a breathtaking 70 per cent decline in newspaper classified advertising between 2000 and 2009, from $19.6 billion to roughly $6 billion according to the Pew Internet Project. When

Newmark and an outfit of thirty people operating out of a small Victorian house in San Francisco cultivated a vast and fully searchable online ecosystem of classified ads they triggered a Darwinian cull of American newspapers. In 2009 alone, 142 American newspapers printed their last paper. Between the beginning of 2008 and the end of 2009, according to an industry blog called Paper Cuts, the industry shed over thirty thousand jobs. When I left Newmark he had the *New York Times* spread out in front of him. At least someone's still reading newspapers, I said. 'I'm an old guy,' he shrugged.

3

If the general-interest newspaper is now an endangered species, so too is the album. Anyone over thirty-five remembers a time when they bought their music in albums from high-street music stores. Back then, singles were only a teaser for the album, and once a band had moved on to selling the next single it was almost impossible to find the previous one anywhere. Not any more. As the universe of music is chopped up into mp3 files and transferred to vast online ecosystems like iTunes, CD album sales remain in the doldrums but singles enjoy something of a renaissance.

In 2009 Americans bought more music than ever before, but sales of albums fell for the fifth year in a row while those of digital singles jumped to 1.16 billion, up 8.3 per cent on the previous year's total, which in turn had been up 27 per cent on the year before that. In Britain, something very similar has been happening. In 2009, according to the British Phonographic Industry, album sales fell for the fifth successive year along with the fortunes of the high-street retailers that sold them. Single sales, however, which are much more likely than albums to be sold as online downloads, continued their steep climb upwards: 89 million singles were sold in the UK in 2007, the following year that figure had risen to 115.1 million and in 2009 they leapt to an all-time high of 152 million. Martin Talbot, the forty-two-year-old music aficionado who spends his time compiling those figures, thinks that the difference from when he was first getting into music is astonishing: 'I remember suddenly getting into David Bowie in the late seventies and the only way to do it was to visit my local record shop on the high street. The selection was pathetic. The only record of his they had in stock was *Ziggy Stardust* – and if they only had one record, that was all you could buy. Plus you had to fork out for the whole album; you were forced into buying a bundle rather than individual tracks. Now, not only can you buy anything that David Bowie has ever recorded, but you can cherry-pick any track you want from any one of Bowie's albums from the thirty-second previews available on sites like Amazon.'

As much as the general-interest newspaper, the album is being dismembered by predatory consumers, cut up into more easily digestible chunks. Each of those chunks is available all of the time, which is more important than you might think. The last time I bought any music, I was sitting in the same coffee bar in Waterloo where I'd met Martin Talbot. Hearing a song I liked but didn't recognise, I took out my iPhone, opened a popular online music recognition application called Shazam and pressed a virtual button. Not only did Shazam correctly establish the name of the song – Pixies' 'Where is My Mind?' from their 1988 album *Surfer Rosa* – but it immediately directed me to its iTunes listing so I could buy it. After a little more button-pressing I was the proud owner of a song that, just a few minutes earlier, I had not even known existed. If I hadn't been able to identify it and purchase it there and then, I probably wouldn't have bothered to buy it at all.

Our predatory approach to electronic information is changing the way that we shop, even for goods that cannot be turned into digital bits and delivered over the internet. Long before the growth of online retailing, we've already seen, the rug was being pulled from underneath general stores like Woolworths. Unlike supermarkets, such shops weren't big enough to develop ecosystems in which people could browse and find anything that they wanted, nor were they small enough to offer a tightly defined range at rock-bottom prices. By arranging similar product categories together in a vast retail environment, shopping malls and out-of-town supermarkets successfully reduced the time we have to spend seeking out all the things that we want – which is why we get so annoyed when they move the stock around. But when everything is tagged with electronic information in a vast virtual universe the effort involved falls much more steeply. The result is that we informavores have become fearless bargain-hunters.

A study by the economist John Morgan and some of his colleagues at the University of California Berkeley found that shoppers who bought electronics products via a price-comparison site saved an average of 16 per cent off the average listed price. The more firms who listed prices, the bigger the savings. Car-buyers who use the internet to research their purchases, according to another study by academics at Yale, pay on average 2.2 per cent less for their cars than those who don't, and that easy access to information on the net has eaten away the average gross profit margin of car-dealers by 22 per cent. And that is only the beginning of it. When our mobile phones allow us to scan products and search for prices and product information elsewhere, the managers of high street stores will be forced to look on powerlessly as hawkish customers stalk their aisles armed with beeping smartphones.

Pricing things up in an instant isn't the only way we're taking advantage of the information we find online. Since vast online ecosystems allow us to pursue exactly what we are after, we are just as likely to spend time truffling for unusual items as hunting out bargains. Whereas the average high-street bookstore contains between forty and one hundred thousand titles, for example, Amazon gives its users instant access to the millions of books in print and millions more that aren't. The freedom to roam and search out anything we want, estimated one study by MIT economists, is seven times more valuable to book-buyers than the lower prices these online retailers make possible. Think about the way in which we use eBay. As much as Craigslist or Amazon, the auction site is a huge online ecosystem that is constantly attracting buyers and sellers. Just like a supermarket, eBay arranges its merchandise in thousands of different categories, but since everything in it is tagged with electronic information most of its users prefer to use its search box rather than browsing. As a result, many of us use it not to pick up the stuff we could get in the supermarket but to track down the distinctive, the unusual and the recherché: a now-defunct toy that we might have played with as a child, a particular part for a computer, a CD we can't find anywhere else.

On eBay, it seems, everyone seems to be on the prowl for something. The first item ever sold there, in 1995, was the site founder Pierre Omidyar's broken laser printer. Amazed that anyone would want to buy it, Omidyar sent the winning bidder an email to make sure he knew what he was buying. 'I'm a collector of broken laser printers,' came the blunt reply. It was not long before the place had been colonised by collectors of unusual items, consumers who are often prepared to pay a premium to land exactly the item they want, and which would be difficult to find anywhere else. David Reiley, an economist who's been studying our behaviour online for more than a decade and who now works for Yahoo! Labs in California, thinks that is only to be expected when an audience is broader but more narrowly focused on its prey. 'In a garage sale,' he explains, 'you're much less likely to find a unique match with what someone really wants. If your old ashtray finds its match in a guy from Idaho who collects hotel ashtrays from the thirties, that's bound to bid the price up.' Hal Varian, Google's chief economist, agrees: 'What's changed,' he told me when I visited him in Google's Mountain View headquarters, 'is the net's incredible ability to bring buyers and sellers together from widely dispersed areas and match them together.' When markets become thicker with more buyers, that is good news for the seller – after all, the only buyer who matters is the one who is prepared to pay the most. The general effect, according to Varian, is that 'costs come down for items that are easily reproduced, but for things that are distinctive in some way we're going to see the opposite – prices are going to go up'. When the item is a genuine one-off, prices can go through the roof. The last bag of Woolworths pick 'n' mix was sold by a former store manager on eBay in February 2009. Following an energetic auction and 115 bids, it went for £14,500.

For us information predators, the experience has been liberating. The ability to compare like for like has turned us into ruthlessly promiscuous shoppers, and has helped to drive down the costs of things that are widely available online. On the other hand, there is some evidence that we are prepared to pay extra to land more distinctive items. For many shoppers, the two might even be related. In 2006, a Boston Consulting Group study of American shoppers concluded that they were consciously spending as little as possible on the basics so that they could pay extra for the high-quality, often unique merchandise – gourmet foods, for example, or boutique home furnishings – that meant a lot to them and which could not be sourced just anywhere. The researchers likened the effect to a treasure hunt, putting the value of the 'trading down' market at $1 trillion a year, and the value of 'trading up' to more distinctive goods at $535 billion. A follow-up study two years later found that the same thing was happening in Brazil, India, Japan and ten European countries.

As we get used to buying things online, our treasure hunt looks certain to gather pace. Over the last few decades many of the mid-range, mainstream products we grew up with have become indistinguishable from their cheaper, generic alternatives. Now all this information at our disposal makes it even easier to slice through the middle in search of either excellent value or distinctive quality. For retailers as much as news organisations, the lesson is that if you can't make a living bulk-selling generic basics, it is better to offer things that some people want very badly and which they cannot readily find anywhere else. In this new retail environment, it does not pay to be caught in the middle.

4

Let's replay the sequence of events that led to my impulse purchase of an obscure Pixies song. Sitting in a coffee bar in Waterloo, I asked an online search engine to fetch the name of a song that I liked the sound of. No sooner had it found it than it directed my attention to iTunes and suggested I buy it. Shazam, the search engine, works by allowing us into its huge universe of information about music – its database recognises eight million songs – and letting us seek out anything we want. But in using it to go straight to the song I was after, I was also letting it in on exactly what I what I was interested in at a precise moment in time. The message Shazam sent back to me was the twenty-first-century version of an old-fashioned classified ad, and it is how the company makes much of its money.

So does Google, but on a much bigger scale. Despite its ambitious schemes to make searchable everything in the world, the company still makes the immense bulk of its billions from the simple text ads that appear at the side of the screen when search results are returned. The reason is simple: it gives advertisers once-unimaginable clues as to our intent. If I search for Hawaii, it is likely that I am interested in holidaying there, and so Google directs my attention to travel agencies and suntan lotions. Politicians are not shy of using it either. During his run for the American presidency, Barack Obama's campaign team spent five million dollars advertising through Google, with much of it on buying up popular search keywords. Anyone who typed 'Barack Muslim' into Google was directed to a page informing viewers that Obama was not a Muslim, while those who typed in 'diabetes' were ushered to a site that informed them that they might not be covered for it under John McCain's healthcare plans. Just like Shazam's prompts to buy the music we have just heard, Google's text ads are really just old-fashioned classified ads that happen to be targeted at the people who really might be interested in them. The result is changing the way in which sellers meet potential buyers, and giving rise to a new kind of intermediary between the two.

By allowing us to forage for what we want, these huge information ecosystems can also track our trail. While we're grazing it is easy to forget about the digital footprints we are leaving behind. The truth is that Craig Newmark was not available to schedule an interview with me, but I ambushed him anyway. By following his movements on Twitter and Foursquare over several months, I discovered that he often visited a coffee bar in San Francisco's Haight-Ashbury district at around half past ten in the morning. Taking a chance, I flew to San Francisco, walked from my hotel to the coffee bar and waited. Ten minutes later, he strolled in and, graciously, invited me to join him rather than calling the police.

Those who control these ecosystems are in an even better position to follow us around. Amazon and eBay already record our buying and browsing histories in order to make recommendations for further purchases. Anyone who signs up for Gmail, Google's email service, agrees to receive small text ads that computers match to the text of their emails. In March 2009 Google unveiled a programme for 'interest-based' advertising or 'behavioural targeting', which goes further – picking up search keywords as we browse around online, even beyond Google. For companies interested in selling us things, the problem with us information predators is that we flit in and out of their websites so quickly that it is difficult for them to get to know who we are. By clubbing together to share information about our movements, or paying companies like Google to follow us around the web, they can build up a more detailed picture of our interests and sprinkle appropriate ads along our path. Car companies, for example, are already doing this, based on reasonable suppositions about behaviour: if, for example, someone types BMW into Google and then reads a motoring column in the *New York Times*, he or she is very likely to be thinking about buying a car. New mothers who have already visited some parenting websites are being presented with advertisements for baby clothes even when they have moved on to do something else online. And not only online. When we leave our computers to move around our towns and cities, the mobile phones in our pockets are using positioning technology to search for their location. With our permission, Google and Twitter already use that location information to follow us around. Google's Latitude application allows us to see the whereabouts of our friends on a map, and mobile applications like Foursquare encourage us to scribble electronic graffiti on anything we encounter along the way.

When just about everything is stamped with electronic information, the city itself will be redrawn as a giant, infinitely searchable information ecosystem. But it also means we will in turn be searchable by the big beasts who are running to catch up with us. One of the inspirations for Frank Woolworth's first 'five and dime' general store in 1879 was a devout Christian called John Wanamaker, who had opened his own store in Philadelphia three years earlier. It was Wanamaker who first began to charge a fixed price for his merchandise to eliminate the need for haggling. He also had the novel idea of buying advertising space in newspapers to promote them, and in 1874 he went beyond the classifieds to place the first-ever half-page ad in a newspaper. 'Half the money I spend on advertising is wasted,' he quipped. 'The trouble is, I don't know which half.' His successors soon will. By darting this way and that in the electronic ether, our awareness becomes so finely grained that it's impossible for any one advertiser to have an exclusive hold on it. For those who can afford it, however, those fine grains yield unprecedented insights into what captures our attention on a minute-by-minute basis. We already think nothing of trading our attention in return for cheap access to newspapers and television programmes. As that attention becomes more difficult to trap, it is likely that we will end up trading our data instead.

The advertising and marketing industries are already excited by the prospect, and with good reason. When their audiences began drifting from them, the big beasts began classifying us into different demographic groups in an attempt to reel us back in. In doing so they hoped to get to know us well enough to predict our behaviour in the near future; most of their attempts to categorise us, however, were blunt instruments. Now they have a much more powerful weapon in their armoury. By mapping up-to-the-minute information about our movements on to data about our income and shopping habits, information ecosystems like Google and Facebook can get a better bead on their audience. It is as if the security guard at Woolworths were suddenly given the nod to follow us around and stamp us with electronic information every time we look at something or check how much its costs – even after we have walked out of the store. By making themselves fully searchable, we saw, ecosystems like Craigslist and eBay allow us information predators to cut through the traditional packages and categories. But that is not all they do. As we move around within them we are also neatly classifying ourselves, making the traditional ways of doing this less and less relevant. 'Search data is the gold standard,' says Google's Hal Varian. 'I don't think you gain a lot by layering demographics on top on that.'

Like Craig Newmark, we are also making it easier to predict

which way we are going to jump next. Sometimes the information trail we leave behind is so routine that those who in control of the data can anticipate our intentions even before we've got the words out; try typing 'weather' into Google and you will probably only get as far as the first couple of letters before it suggests the forecast for your local city. Furthermore, by unearthing hidden connections between our different trails they sometimes get to know what we want before we're even aware of it ourselves. In 2006 a New York behavioural targeting firm called Tacoda discovered that the group most likely to rent a car were not those who had searched the internet for rental cars, but those who had recently read an obituary online. 'Consumers may know things they think they want,' the company's founder Dave Morgan told *Advertising Age* in 2008, 'but they don't know for sure what they might want. They're not spending all their time hunting for those things.' What they might want to do next, of course, is not always as benign as renting a car. Think about that suicidal teenager in Oxford. The way that he had filled out his Facebook profile was enough to take police officers as far as his school; to get any closer they resorted to Google. But that was not the only electronic trail the boy left behind. If someone had had full access to his computer in the week before his suicide attempt, they would have been aware of his interest in suicide websites. Of course, not everyone who visits such sites is contemplating suicide, and few of us would want to hand this kind of information over to the police. What is striking, though, is how accurate it turned out to be. If the different tracks the boy left behind had been put together and the necessary connections made, it would have told the authorities just about all they needed to know.

*

When everything is branded with electronic information and released into a giant online ecosystem, it is so much easier for information predators to home in on exactly what we are after. But the game goes both ways. Just as we use search engines, the information trail we leave behind makes it easy to find out what we are like and which way we're headed.

For the big beasts who have woken up in this strange new environment, all this has come as quite a shock. They had grown used to controlling the middle ground. Their middlebrow fare, however, isn't looking as wholesome as it once was. In any case, it makes little sense to offer the public a generalised selection when it can simply pick it apart and make off with whatever it wants. If they persist in trying to cover the whole beach-front, in trying to be all things to everyone, they risk being swept away in a sea of online information. They can certainly work with those who control information ecosystems to keep track of how we move around them, but they also need to be able to offer us something more distinctive. This is not as daunting as it sounds. Just because we information predators can narrow our field of attention, it does not mean that we're spending all our time snacking on the obscure and the recherché. Not everyone can get by on old Pixies songs. With such a rich menu to choose from, our diet is simply growing more diverse. So are the ways in which we come across it. Constantly foraging for ourselves can be exhausting work. That is why we stick together in flocks and, by passing around information among ourselves, find out which way to fly and what is good to eat. First of all, though, we need to find something worth passing around.

5

The New Nesting Places

From blockbuster to niche-buster

On the new things growing up all around us

In the autumn of 1995, just a few months into his new job as head of programming for the American cable channel HBO, Chris Albrecht gathered the company's executives together for a meeting. 'All right,' he said, 'let me ask a question: do we really believe that we are who we say we are? This distinctive, high-quality, edgy, worth-paying-for service?' The long silence that followed confirmed his view about what HBO needed to do next. For the previous decade, the channel had been sprinkling into its schedule of first-run Hollywood films and boxing matches some original programming – live comedy, documentaries and the occasional sitcom. As the number of cable channels grew, however, Home Box Office wasn't the only place viewers could go to watch films before they arrived on free-to-air broadcast television. Others were popping up to offer live sports and shows too. What HBO lacked was an elusive ingredient that would lead viewers to them, and them only. Missing, as Albrecht put it, 'was a real grown-up plan of how to build an outstanding one-of-a-kind programming service'.

Albrecht's loaded question was all the more remarkable because, until 1995, his company had been doing rather well. HBO had opened for business on 8 November 1972, the invention of a Long Island entrepreneur called Charles Dolan. Its first transmission schedule comprised the Paul Newman film *Sometimes a Great Notion* and an ice hockey game between the New York Rangers and the Vancouver Canucks; only 365 cable TV subscribers, all of them from the single city of Wilkes-Barre in north-eastern Pennsylvania, signed up to see it. There was no reason why anyone should. American network television was so flush with advertising that it had been free to air for thirty years. During the hours in which Americans sat on the sofa watching them, the three television networks – CBS, NBC and ABC – could claim an exclusive hold on their attention, and so the commercial breaks were sold for vast sums of money. Pitted against these existing big beasts of television, HBO knew that it could not compete. But if it could supplement its diet with something that people really wanted to see, that they would not be able to see elsewhere, Dolan reckoned, some of them might be prepared to pay for the privilege. At first that something was television premieres of Hollywood films and live access to sporting events, music concerts and stand-up comedy.

The company's first live satellite transmission aired on 1 October 1975, after HBO negotiated exclusive rights to stream the world-title fight between Muhammad Ali and Joe Frazier. The 'Thrilla in Manila' immediately became the stuff of legend and overnight HBO became a channel worth watching. In 1976 alone subscriptions leapt from 15,000 to 287,199; by the end of 1977 HBO had six hundred thousand subscribers and had turned a profit for the first time. By the following decade it was buying up the rights to Richard Pryor gigs and Barbra Streisand concerts, and was signing up subscribers at a terrific pace: when Albrecht arrived at the company in 1985, it had 14.6 million of them. HBO also began to dabble in making its own shows, turning out a few well-regarded documentaries and quirky sit-coms in the late eighties and early nineties.

It was in the early nineties, however, that the growth in HBO subscribers began to stall. Other cable companies were moving on to its turf. Showtime, for example, was launched in 1976 and set about broadcasting live concerts and films before they appeared on the mainstream networks. In 1995, with subscriptions lying flat at just over 19 million, HBO's management decided it was time for a change, which is how Chris Albrecht had come to win his promotion. Albrecht, a dome-headed man in his early forties who looked more like a club bouncer than a television executive, had a reputation for being bullishly supportive of writers and programme-makers that he respected. Together with his well-regarded production chief Carolyn Strauss, he set about turning HBO into a haven for the highest-quality television drama that money could buy. Albrecht raised the budget for original programming from $50 million to $300 million a year. He doubled the money available for programme development – television's equivalent of R&D – to $4 million per prime-time hour. He cut back the channel's programming output to make sure that only the best programmes would get made.

Most controversial of all was his resolve to give his writers free rein. One of Albrecht's first creative decisions in his new job was to go back to Tom Fontana, a writer that HBO had been toying with by demanding endless rewrites of his script for a drama series. 'We've really screwed up your idea,' Albrecht remembers telling him. 'Here's a million dollars. Go give us your vision of what the show is going to be.' Two years later Fontana came back with a gritty prison drama called *Oz*. With its unabashed portrayal of prison homosexuality, violence, gangs and rape, *Oz* would have been impossible to air on American network television. It did, however, win a devoted army of fans on cable, and its success inspired other writers to think about what television could do. One of those writers was David Chase, who had been hustling his idea about a vicious New Jersey mobster in the throes of a mid-life crisis around the broadcast TV networks for some time. After a good deal of persuading, Albrecht agreed to commission a pilot. He didn't much like the scene where the mobster takes time out from ferrying his daughter around prospective colleges to garrotte a police informer. He and his executives weren't thrilled with the title either: *The Sopranos*, they felt, made it sound like a minority-interest opera documentary. But Chase refused to budge and Albrecht eventually caved in and let him do it the way he wanted. The first series of *The Sopranos* aired in January 1999 to immediate and thunderous acclaim. The *New York Times* thought that it might be 'the greatest work of American popular culture of the last quarter-century'.

Television would never be the same again. *The Sopranos* had started solidly with an audience of 7.5 million; by the third series it had grown to 11.3 million viewers, and by the time the fourth series aired in 2002 it was pulling in 13.4 million. It was the first series to draw audiences large enough to be comparable to the broadcast networks, one critic noting drily that HBO now had on its hands 'the first television megahit ever to be unavailable to the majority of viewers'. Its success also taught both Albrecht and HBO a valuable lesson: that there was money to be made by putting writers in charge rather than attempting to second-guess them at every turn. It wasn't just *The Sopranos*. *Sex and the City* had arrived in 1998 and won an avid audience for its frank, female-friendly conversation about sex and relationships. In 2000 came *Curb Your Enthusiasm*, Larry David's partially improvised and wholly scatological play on his misanthropic alter ego. As the hits rolled out HBO began to chalk up record-breaking profits for its parent company Time Warner; in 2001 alone it made $700 million in profits on $2.5 billion revenues. When Albrecht ploughed some of those profits back into hiring the best available talent, and word got out that writers were well-treated at HBO, the momentum became unstoppable. Between 1996 and 2001, the share of HBO's schedule devoted to original programmes rose from 25 per cent to 40 per cent. The channel had deliberately set itself up, according to Albrecht, 'as a place where creative people can cover and do their best work. We are the patrons of these terrifically talented people.'

HBO had found what it was looking for, a steady diet of highest-quality original drama that viewers would not be able to find anywhere else, and which they might be prepared to pay for. And not just any high-quality drama. Left to their own devices, Albrecht began to realise, writers and programme-makers were more likely to come up with ground-breaking television that explored the changing dynamics of family and society in fresh and challenging new ways. 'HBO had decided to put their faith in David Chase,' says Matt Weiner, the creator of *Mad Men* who also wrote for *The Sopranos*. 'From then on . . .

they would allow the creators of the shows to pursue their own visions. They realised that was the only way to make shows that were truly unique.' In encouraging its writers to make the most of their freedom, HBO took great pains to define itself against mainstream network television. 'I just want to be in a show where I can say "fuck",' says one of the characters in *Curb Your Enthusiasm*. If the show's success is anything to go by, many Americans seem to know how she feels. HBO shows seem to revel in the kind of sex, profanity and violence that could never be shown on the tightly regulated broadcast channels; to get them repeated on mainstream networks, HBO often gets its actors to dub over their work with alternatives to the original swearing. Since 1996, the network's tagline has been 'It's not TV, it's HBO', an approach the academic Marc Leverette has dubbed the 'cocksucker, motherfucker, tits' philosophy of television. By the time Alan Ball showed up in 2001 with a darkly humorous script set in a Los Angeles funeral parlour, the only question that came back from HBO's executives was, 'Can you make it more fucked-up?'

It wasn't just the fucks, of course, that kept HBO viewers coming back for more. When stories can be told in instalments over fifty or sixty hours, it changes the kinds of stories television is capable of telling. In 2002 Albrecht was appointed chairman and CEO of HBO, and in the same year he unveiled *The Wire*, an epic of crime, poverty and collateral punishment in post-industrial Baltimore. Like many other HBO shows, *The Wire* made no sense in small doses – it was wilfully cryptic and deliberately baffled the casual viewer with its slang and its rapidly expanding canvas. In doing so it helped propagate the notion that television need not be trashy and forgettable; that, as much as a novel, television could demand a certain investment of time and reward viewers by drawing them further into its world.

'The first season of *The Wire* was a training exercise,' its creator David Simon has said. 'We were training you to watch television differently.' He was also cultivating a different kind of audience. Mainstream, middlebrow television used to pride itself on its ability to simplify things for the average viewer, but David Simon made it clear that he has no patience for it. In an interview with the *Guardian*, he explained his philosophy in traditional HBO house style: 'Fuck the average viewer.' He was deliberately turning away casual viewers who need everything explained to them, the very audience HBO had traditionally relied upon. The network had appealed to those who would use it only occasionally, because they really wanted to see a new film or a high-profile concert, but both Simon and Albrecht felt that this was no longer enough. 'We knew that we had to become even more valuable,' Albrecht told the *Hollywood Reporter* in 2002, 'so we made a conscious effort to explore the series areas, and then we talked and we said, "Look, we need to anchor these things because it's too hard to find them." So we've transformed into a regular-use network, a habitual-use network, rather than an occasional-use network – and I think that has been a huge transformation but one that was necessary.' HBO, says the academic John Thornton Caldwell, remade itself as 'boutique television', imbuing its shows with 'an air of selectivity, refinement, uniqueness and privilege' so that viewers would keep coming back. The gamble paid off. By 2004 HBO was raking in more than a billion dollars a year in profit, one of the biggest yields taken by any channel in the history of television. In less than a decade it had become the greatest single producer of original drama in the English-speaking world.

HBO now sells its programmes to 150 countries around the world. By 2004 it was nudging thirty million American subscribers, where it has hovered ever since. Chris Albrecht succeeded because he realised that, in the new television ecosystem that was then materialising, everything was up for grabs. Armed with remote controls, VCRs and digital video recorders, television viewers were becoming more hawkish in their television-watching. When Albrecht took the plunge and used a certain kind of high-quality television to define his output, he carved out a distinctive niche for HBO. Just like us information predators, he successfully narrowed his channel's field of attention. But he did not just want to invite us in for a snack; his plan was to steal away our attention for much longer by offering us a richer and more nutritious meal. In doing so, he created a new kind of nesting place where original television could grow.

2

Chris Albrecht and HBO played their hand well, but their gambit would not have worked without changes that were happening all around them. Between the fifties and seventies, the 'big three' American broadcast networks were just about all there was to watch. Together they took 90 per cent of the prime-time audience; popular shows could attract as many as 70 per cent of the available viewers. But with the proliferation of cable outlets like HBO – the number of channels a typical American household could receive jumped from 7.2 channels in 1970 to 96.4 in 2005 – together with an increase in the time that we spend watching things online, their audience has been leaking away for the last thirty years. During the 2004–2005 television season, only 32 per cent of American viewers – fewer than one in three households – were tuned to ABC, CBS, or NBC during prime-time periods. Much the same has been happening in the UK. Between 1999 and 2008, the proportion of the audience lured away from the main broadcast networks by newer cable or satellite stations grew from 14 per cent to 38.8. For years now the two main terrestrial channels, BBC1 and ITV, have been watching their audiences dwindle. On both sides of the Atlantic there are now so many channels that TV critics are becoming an endangered species. After all, argue editors, what's the point of reviewing a single programme when so few readers will have seen it?

From life in a small pond, the big fish of broadcast television now find themselves adrift in a vast ocean of digital information. As much as General Motors and the newspaper industry, they've been thrown into a hostile new environment, one in which they no longer have an exclusive hold on our attention. Just like them, the television networks have responded by fighting a desperate rearguard action. Beginning in the nineties, they set about targeting their shows more precisely at the juiciest parts of the audience so they could sell them on to sponsors, which often led to 'cookie-cutter' shows that tried too hard to flatter their audiences. They aggressively cut their costs, slashing budgets, firing workers, showing more repeats and bulking up on advertising: after a period of industry deregulation, the average time set aside for commercials on American network television increased from six minutes and forty-eight seconds per hour in 1982 to twelve minutes and four seconds in 2001. They also began to spread their prime-time programming very thin in an effort to halt the slide in their ratings. In the summer of 2000, when ABC had an enormously successful run broadcasting *Who Wants To Be A Millionaire?* four times a week, the other networks rushed to followed suit with their own game shows. Before long they had all become addicted to the same diet of 'big event' programmes – game shows, reality TV such as *Survivor* and *Big Brother*, and talent competitions like *American Idol* and *The X-Factor*. The formula seems to work. In Britain in May 2009 the final of the third series of *Britain's Got Talent* – featuring Susan Boyle, the bashful Scottish singer whose earlier performance on the programme had turned her into an overnight sensation – attracted 19.2 million viewers, a 68 per cent share of the audience that made it the highest-rating show on British television in five years. *American Idol*, meanwhile, has become one of the most popular shows ever made; between 2004 and 2009 it was the most watched series on any American network. Shows like this, a report from the American Federal Communications Commission has noted, are much cheaper to produce than scripted programmes. They can also be very lucrative. As mainstream culture cracks up, they offer a valuable opportunity for advertisers to set aside their targeting armoury and reach everyone at the same time. Prime-time evening television has always been about entertaining audiences in large numbers. Buffeted by competition in a vast new television ecosystem, however, its big beasts have all gravitated towards exactly the same inexpensive formula and as a result their output has become interchangeably generic. In November 2010 ITV's chairman Archie Norman complained that his channel had become stuck in a 'ratings rat race' in its thirst for mass audiences, which had driven it 'to the lowest common denominator'. A week later the BBC's governing body, the BBC Trust, admitted that much of the programming on its main channels had become 'formulaic and derivative', and was damaging its reputation. Lit up by the likes of Simon Cowell, Piers Morgan and Donald Trump, prime-time television has become a ghostly presence in the corner of the room. Desperate to hang on to its audience, it has sunk to the very lowest common denominator.

It is also a shadow of its former self. As hawkish viewers get used to watching things whenever and however they want via digital video recorders, prime-time TV is being pulled apart by its audience. In autumn 2009, when NBC executives decided to move the talk-show host Jay Leno from the *Tonight Show*, which airs at 11.35 p.m., to an earlier slot at ten o'clock, they were betting that the topicality of the show would mean that viewers would want to watch it there and then. Instead, many chose that hour to feast on all the prime-time fare they had stored up on their TiVo boxes and give both Jay Leno and the other channels a miss. In January 2010 NBC cancelled the experiment, and returned Leno to his original home on the *Tonight Show*. Even more confusing for the big beasts, their prime cuts are routinely being filleted on the net. 'I've always wanted to perform in front of a large audience,' Susan Boyle told the presenters before her debut performance on *Britain's Got Talent* in April 2009. It turned out to be bigger that she imagined: the television audience of twelve million was dwarfed by the hundred million scattered around the world who watched the five-minute internet clip of her singing 'I Dreamed a Dream'. As it made its way around the net that clip was edited in very different ways – people even took to watching clips of other people watching it and it became the most popular video ever watched on YouTube. Bite-sized clips like this are perfect for watching on video-sharing sites. More than 170 million American watched an average of 182 videos online in November 2009, but the average length of those videos was just four minutes. Perhaps as a result, an incredible mass of esoteric interests are now being sated on the internet, many of which we didn't even know had an audience.

In his 2006 book *The Long Tail* Chris Anderson, editor-in-chief of *Wired* magazine, tried to make sense of all this. With limited space on their shelves, Anderson argued, high-street stores usually relied on a few books or films that they could shift in huge quantities. But when just about anything can be picked out from an infinite electronic shelf, that lack of space ceases to be an issue. As a consequence, Anderson predicted, sales would move away from the small number of hits at the head of the sales curve towards the mass of minnows that make up its 'long tail'. The monopoly of the blockbuster was over, said Anderson. The future lay in 'the mass of niches' – a huge uncharted expanse consisting of all the obscure stuff that was previously uneconomic to sell. But that is not really what happened. Anderson was inspired by places like Amazon and eBay. Not everyone, however, can morph into a huge beast with a long tail. Even if they could, it probably would not amount to much.

In 2008, a study of how people buy music and DVDs online in America and Australia undertaken by Harvard Business School professor Anita Elberse found that blockbusters were more dominant than ever. The long tail was certainly there – larger numbers of books and music were being made available than ever before – but they were being put out faster than we could discover them, and the result was that those at the top were taking a bigger share than ever. Later in the same year, a study of online music sales in Britain discovered that more than ten million of the thirteen million singles made available on the internet in the previous year had failed to find a single buyer; four-fifths of all sales had come from the most popular fifty-two thousand tracks. Much the same has happened with television. As audiences drifted away from the American broadcast networks, Chris Anderson felt sure that they would end up sliding down the long tail in very different directions. But, with an average of 96.4 channels to choose from in 2005, American viewers spent the vast majority of their time watching just 16.3 of them: the broadcast networks plus MTV, HBO, CNN and a handful of others. Just because we information predators can have anything we want whenever we want it, does not mean that we all want to eat different things. With an unlimited menu to choose from, we are huddling together in large groups rather than going off on our own. And as new things to watch sprout up, our diet is growing more diverse. The same people who snack on bite-sized nuggets of online video at work might take in a long serial like *The Wire* an episode at a time in the evening, a richer and more satisfying story than anything they are likely to encounter on mainstream television. Just as novels evolved in the nineteenth century to cope with the demands of newspaper serialisation, television in our new environment is slowly liberating itself from the stale old one-hour or two-hour formats. And not only TV. As music gets produced for storage in vast online ecosystems, the technology writer Steven Johnson has pointed out, songs are slowly stretching out beyond the usual three-minute mark. As we get used to downloading them on to our Kindles and iPads we can expect books to follow suit, putting an end to the Gutenberg era in which ideas of all kinds were forced to squeeze themselves into seventy thousand words.

Dividing the culture we consume into blockbusters at one end and minnows at the other does not really do justice to the strange things that happen when mainstream culture collapses beneath us. As middlebrow television disintegrates and a new ecosystem grows up around it, one effect is that audiences migrate to shared nesting places where they are not likely to be disturbed. Just before Christmas 2009 I found myself in a cinema in London's Mayfair waiting for the curtain to go up on New York's Metropolitan Opera. While I sat amid a sea of gregarious mink coats, the digital screen panned around the audience in New York and relayed its murmur of expectation back to us in London. Four hours long and featuring an orchestra, nudity and subtitles, a live transmission of *Les contes d'Hoffmann* plainly isn't for everyone. Nor was the experience flawless: we in London strained to know when to applaud, for example, or when to rise for the interval. To an opera novice like me, however, it was utterly captivating.

Watching opera via live broadcast, of course, is nothing new. In 1950 NBC commissioned an Italian-American composer called Gian Carlo Menotti to write the first opera ever to be commissioned for television. Menotti wasn't wholly convinced by the idea, and was at a loss to know what to write. While wandering through New York's Metropolitan Museum, however, legend has it that he chanced upon a Hieronymus Bosch painting of the Nativity and found immediate inspiration. The result, the one-act *Amahl and the Night Visitors*, was performed for the first time on Christmas Eve 1951 at New York City's Rockefeller Center and broadcast live on prime-time television to an audience of five million – still the largest-ever audience to watch an opera on television. For the next fifteen years, *Amahl* became a staple of the NBC Christmas schedule. Following suit, the BBC made several productions of it for British audiences. By the late seventies, however, opera and classical music more generally had largely been abandoned by mainstream network television. 'In the fifties,' the *New Yorker*'s classical music critic Alex Ross told me, 'there was a sense among those running the networks that opera deserved our attention, that it needed to be invested in. But by the late seventies, all they were interested in was the biggest possible audiences. That was something opera was never going to have, and so opera and classical music simply disappeared.'

While national broadcast television has been retreating from its traditional middlebrow mission, many of those things are turning up in whole new nesting places – in digital cinemas, on cable and on the internet. Since 2006, at the instigation of its arriving general manager Peter Gelb, the New York Metropolitan Opera has been broadcasting operas live and in high definition. In the course of its 2009–10 season alone, opera at the Met played to over 868 cinemas all over the world; 2.2 million people in forty-four countries watched a total of nine operas, many more than the eight hundred thousand who came to see them at the company's New York home. The Met takes half of all the revenues, Gelb told me, and it is already making a profit from the scheme. Similarly, as the arts find themselves squeezed out of broadcast television in Britain – arts programming now accounts for just 3 per cent of airtime on the four main broadcast networks, according to the industry regulator Ofcom – major theatres and art galleries are stepping into the breach by transmitting live broadcasts and internet documentaries to enthusiastic audiences around the world. Culture vultures are not the only ones to enjoy uninterrupted access to their favourite events. When in 2009 the embattled BBC was forced to pull out of covering Crufts dog show amid a storm of publicity over animal rights, an independent production company called Sunset+Vine arrived at a deal to stream live and wholly uninterrupted coverage of the event direct over the net to 'dog-lovers worldwide'. One hundred and forty-seven thousand tuned in to watch it. For Sunset+Vine as much as for the New York Metropolitan Opera or HBO, this ability to bypass mainstream television is often a liberating experience. No longer do they have to make any concessions to mainstream taste or sensitivities. Nor do they need to edit their material to the attention-span of the average viewer; instead, they attract an audience of passionate enthusiasts who will gorge on it for as long as they like.

As new stuff grows around us in this new television ecosystem, it is likely that the prices that we will have to pay for it will vary to match the meal. At twenty-five pounds, that opera I saw was twice as expensive as watching a film in the same cinema – then again, it was more than twice as long as the average film. With more of us becoming culturally omnivorous, there is no reason why we should not drift from one nesting place to another and sample everything on the menu. Just because someone watches *American Idol* or *Britain's Got Talent* does not mean that they are not a dog-lover, high-end drama enthusiast and an opera buff too. But they are only likely to be willing to pay for the stuff that they really want, and which they can't find for free elsewhere.

3

There is something else striking about the stuff which is managing to grow in this new television ecosystem. Dog shows, live opera broadcasts, drama serials as long and richly textured as Victorian novels – all define themselves much more on what they can offer us rather than on the make-up of their audience. That might sound obvious, but it is very different from what many of the big beasts of mainstream culture have been up to for the last few decades. Faced with escaping audiences, they responded by training their sights more firmly on the characteristics of that audience. Some tried to lump us all together and head straight for the lowest common denominator, while others split us up into different species so that they could go after us one at a time. They were hoping to find our new nesting places. It didn't always work, and sometimes it made matters worse. These new nesting places do the opposite. Rather than slicing us up into different groups, they start out by making their product different. Think about what happened at HBO. Instead of sinking to the lowest common denominator, or seeking common denominators in the audience, HBO found its common denominators in its product and then used them to attract an enthusiastic audience. While the broadcast networks were busy using bean-counters and data-gatherers to hunt out an audience, HBO did not seem to care where its audience came from or what it looked like. Asked by an industry reporter to characterise his audience in 2001, Chris Albrecht pleaded ignorance: 'We have a very broad subscriber base that is slightly more upscale than a broadcast network audience. But without knowing exactly what our subscribers are – and we don't, because we're not exactly provided that information by the cable companies – it's very hard for us to actually make a statement one way or the other.' Rather than seeking to differentiate its audience it made its product different, and an avidly enthusiastic audience gathered around it.

In the pharmaceuticals industry they have invented a word for this: 'niche-buster'. Among the first to use it was a young Indian analyst called Shabeer Hussain, and one afternoon I visited him in his offices in London to ask him what he meant by it. Hussain delivered a whistle-stop history of his industry from Alexander

Fleming's chance discovery of penicillin in his Petri dish in 1928 to the present day. Beginning in the early eighties, he told me, the big beasts of the drugs industry were expanding and gobbling up smaller companies at a ferocious rate. They also began to lean more heavily on a small handful of blockbusters to deliver the lion's share of their revenues. In the drugs industry a blockbuster is usually defined as one that takes a billion dollars a year in revenues. To make that kind of money, drug companies have traditionally aimed at diseases widespread in the general population: cardiovascular problems like heart disease, for example, which might affect nearly half of the world's population at some point in their lives. Pfizer's cholesterol-reducing drug Lipitor was a gargantuan blockbuster, making £12 billion in sales in 2008 and becoming the biggest-selling prescription drug in the world.

Trying to turn out blockbusters is, however, a risky business. Drug companies get between eighteen and twenty years' protection for their inventions under patent law, but about half of that is taken up with laboratory work to develop the drug and the laborious and hugely expensive business of organising clinical trials. Precious few drugs make it out the other end. Those that do must race to make their money back before their patent protection expires and other manufacturers arrive to produce much cheaper, generic versions of the same thing. Lipitor, for example, loses patent protection in 2011. As their blockbusters neared the end of patent protection, Hussain told me, many of the big beasts of pharmaceuticals started to tweak their function to extend their patent protection or expand their market – making them look fresher and more hard-hitting, for example, or useful for a broader range of complaints. As Viagra approached the end of its patent Pfizer sought regulatory approval to use the same chemical, in a lower dose and renamed Revatio, for the rare lung condition pulmonary hypertension. Other companies began to churn out drugs that were not very new at all; so-called 'me too' drugs that work on the same diseases in very similar ways. To distinguish their drugs from similar competitors and prepare them for the arrival of generic alternatives, big pharmaceutical companies have also spent very aggressively on marketing and branding, targeting their drugs in different ways to different audiences to make them stand out. In 2004, for example, AstraZeneca spent $216 million promoting its own cholesterol-reducing drug Crestor, four million dollars more than Pepsi spent on marketing its products in the same year.

Not every drug company has been moving in this direction. A few have chosen to investigate so-called orphan diseases, genetically inherited complaints that affect only a few thousand people scattered around the world. Take Gaucher's disease, says Shabeer Hussain. Gaucher's disease is a very rare hereditary enzyme deficiency that afflicts about ten thousand people worldwide, most of them Ashkenazi Jews. In the early nineties Genzyme, a small Massachusetts-based biotechnology company set up specifically to look into orphan diseases, developed a new enzyme replacement therapy with which to treat it. By 2008 Cerezyme was making $1.24 billion a year for its manufacturers, a huge sum of money for a drug that was only being used by five thousand patients. The big beasts have been taking note and are now coming up with niche-busters of their own.

It is not hard to see why. Since niche-busters are generally much more complicated to produce than other drugs – the production lines are more sophisticated, the patients can be anywhere in the world and the drugs themselves are usually injected rather than swallowed – it is more difficult for a generic manufacturer to copy them. Neither, since the diseases themselves are very rare, is there any point in advertising them via mainstream channels. A niche-buster succeeds by taking a rifle-shot to overlooked therapeutic areas; instead of flattering or badgering people into buying it, it gets by on the distinctiveness of its product. It can afford to. With no need to puff up its brand, it can spend much more to ensure that its product is really effective: a niche-buster might plough up to 60 or 70 per cent of its revenues back into research and development compared to only 20 to 25 per cent for a blockbuster drug. With something truly distinctive to offer it can attract a small group of people who badly need its help, and charge a great deal for this. Treatment with Cerezyme costs about a quarter of a million dollars a year (the treatment is usually picked up by insurers). In 2010 niche-busters accounted for $66 billion, or 7 to 8 per cent of total pharmaceutical industry revenues; those figures, Shabeer Hussain believes, are certain to keep going up.

In the drugs industry as much as television, niche-busters are evolving into the new blockbusters. It is hardly surprising. Blockbuster drugs have become something of a liability – expensive and hugely risky, and prone to falling flat on their face. What niche-busters like Genzyme do is very different. As much as HBO, they base their products not on the demographic characteristics of their audience but on something distinctive they have to offer it. By narrowing their field of attention they have managed to attract modest but highly enthusiastic customers, many of whom are happy to come from far afield because they were unable find anything like them elsewhere. By concentrating all their efforts on satisfying those audiences, both HBO and the pharmaceutical niche-busters have allowed their produce time to breathe and develop. What is more, their insistence on the uniqueness of their fare – 'It's not TV. It's HBO' – forces them to take risks and plough some of their profits back into developing original work.

4

While the big beasts of the film industry flounder, a few niche-busters are growing up under their feet. The notion of the film blockbuster, as we saw at the beginning of this book, only really dates from 1975 and the arrival of *Jaws*. Blockbusters were big, noisy ventures designed to appeal to just about everyone and repay the studio's huge investment by cleaning up at the box office. By the turn of the century, however, most of them had degenerated into joyless franchises. Just like the drugs companies, the Hollywood studios began tweaking their films into samey sequels, turning out the same dull, formulaic fare as everyone else. They also resorted to target practice, manufacturing films specifically to sate the appetite of the all-important teenage audience. In the last decade, however, the big beasts of the film industry have found themselves in a hostile new environment, one in which video games, pirated DVDs and the internet all vie for attention. Not only that, but boutique television producers have been muscling in, stealing their thunder with stories richer and more rewarding than anything that can be fitted into a two-hour film. With its dedication to the maverick vision of its writers and producers, and its commitment to original work, HBO has inherited much of the mantle of an old-fashioned Hollywood studio. 'I think a lot of people have given up on the movies,' says the film critic David Thomson. 'The truth is that television, if you pick and choose, is a lot more grown-up and satisfying these days, beginning with HBO.'

Many of us continue to go to the cinema to watch films, if only for the experience of sitting in the dark beside someone we like. For the Hollywood studios, the bigger problem is the growing expense of making them. One of the essential ingredients of the blockbuster, says Chris Anderson in *The Long Tail*, is the biggest Hollywood star that can possibly be signed up. It used to be that landing a big Hollywood hitter like Tom Cruise – for a romantic comedy like *Cocktail*, an action film like *Mission: Impossible* or a sci-fi mystery like *Vanilla Sky* – could virtually guarantee success at the box office. In return, the star could command a huge fee: Cruise was one of a small group of megastars known as the $20 million club.

For over a decade, a slightly nerdy academic in his late fifties has been waging a lonely, one-man guerrilla war on the $20 million club. S. Abraham Ravid is not the average film-industry pundit. He is a professor of finance at Rutgers University in New Jersey, and in the late nineties he became fascinated by the often torturously labyrinthine process of financing films. When Ravid ran Hollywood's numbers through his data-crunching techniques he found some disturbing flaws in their logic. In one study he took a random sample of 175 films that had been made in the nineties and ranked them according to their stars and how much money they made. What came out the other end surprised him: big-budget films often made lots of money at the box office, but spending a huge amount on a star made no perceptible difference. So why spend the money? Ravid had an answer for that, too. According to him, the employment of a bankable star is a form of economic signalling, an intimation to the audience that the studio knows something that they don't. 'If I sell my house to put my money into a pizza parlour,' says Ravid, 'that signals my confidence that I make very good pizza. In the same way, when I pay huge amounts of money for a star, I'm signalling to everyone that the film must have something going for it.' Like a blockbuster brand-name drug that costs much more than its generic equivalent, film stars had became trusted brands – guarantees of quality before anyone has had a chance to sample the product. For Hollywood's executives, they'd also become useful insurance policies. 'The truth is, if I made a film with you and me as the stars, I'd be out on the street with a picture of my kids in my hand. But if I hire Tom Cruise or Julia Roberts, at worst I might get an initial bump and a few reviews. And if the film subsequently flops, I can always throw up my hands and say "who knew"?' The result, Ravid believes, has encouraged a herd mentality among the studio chiefs, in which everyone plumps for the same expensive stars because they are afraid of losing their jobs.

Avri Ravid did his best to spread the word about his research and its implications. He even wrote to the letters page of the *New York Times*, solemnly informing the studios that they were wasting huge amounts of money. For a long time, no one paid much attention; in the summer of 2009, however, his phone began to ring. The *New York Times* wanted to canvass his opinion on the industry, and some senior Hollywood executives wanted to invite him in to talk about his research. The reason wasn't hard to fathom: the signalling function of the $20 million club seemed to have stopped working. The summer of 2009 was calamitous for both Hollywood film stars and traditional blockbusters. The biggest hits were the robot film *Transformers: Revenge of the Fallen*, Pixar's computer-animated comedy *Up*, *Harry Potter and the Half-Blood Prince* and *New Moon*, the latest in the *Twilight* vampire saga. None of these films showcased any really big Hollywood stars. Worse, those that did – Johnny

Depp's *Public Enemies*, for instance – made meagre returns at the box office. 'The cratering of films with big stars is astounding,' Peter Guber, the former chairman of Sony, told the *New York Times*. 'These super-talented people are failing to aggregate a large audience, and everybody is looking for answers.'

As the $20 million club loses its lustre, the see-saw of risk versus reward in the Hollywood studios is subtly shifting. On the one hand, 'big event' films can still make massive amounts of money, even without paying through the nose for Hollywood stars. They are, however, prohibitively expensive to make and deeply dicey, with plenty more misses than hits. To do these kind of films properly, another study by Avri Ravid and some colleagues concluded, the studios are increasingly partnering up to share the costs and spread the risk. James Cameron's *Titanic* turned out to be so expensive that its owners at 20th Century Fox were forced to join forces with Paramount to avoid being sunk by its rapidly advancing costs. By the time it came to back *Avatar*, Fox had learned to hedge its bets by sharing the risks with outside financial investors. *Avatar* arrived with an estimated price-tag of half a billion dollars, and even then it did not boast a single recognisable star. In order to recoup the huge investment, such films need to attract an audience from every corner of the world. To do so, they must stretch themselves very thin: *Avatar*, for example, is possessed of such shamelessly global ambitions that any nuances of character and story seem to have been deliberately ironed out. Another way into 'big event' films is to replace film stars with superheroes. Comic-book characters like Spider-Man, notes *The Economist*, dominate cinema screens just as did Steven Spielberg's eighties blockbusters or the star-driven vehicles of the nineties. For studio moguls, the advantage of superheroes is that they play to familiar audiences, and the little-known actors who play them can be hired cheaply. They are not, after all, the stars of the show.

The riskiness of movie blockbusters is one reason why some Hollywood big beasts are now fighting for their survival: in November 2010 MGM, the debt-laden studio behind *Gone with the Wind*, filed for bankruptcy protection in a plan that would see it rescued by a small production company called Spyglass Entertainment. It also explains why many of them, as well as putting some of their eggs in the basket of a few 'big event' films, are seeking out more dependable nesting places. In Chapter 3 we saw how they've quietly colonised art-house cinema, though art-house isn't the only genre they're moving into. There is also a growing market for horror. Blockbusters, at least the early ones like *Jaws*, were made for almost everyone; with the widest possible audience, they were more likely to do big business at the box office. From the eighties onwards, the studios generally assumed that the widest possible audience could be had by aiming at the PG13 certificate. For some time now, film-industry academics have been scratching their heads over why studios are producing such a glut of horror films, which come with an R rating (an 18 rating in the UK). Some have even dubbed it the 'R-rated puzzle': after all, if sex and violence narrow the range of the audience so drastically, why bother making horror movies at all? The answer, Avri Ravid concluded in yet another of his studies, is that they have become a less risky bet for movie executives who do not want to lose their shirt. Low-budget horror is unlikely to make studios a fortune, but it is not going to lose them huge sums of money either. Horror franchises like *Scream*, Ravid points out, don't need a big star to succeed: 'Who remembers any of the actors in

Nightmare on Elm Street?' Then there is the fact that, unlike comedy and romance, sex and violence easily transcend cultural barriers. When a visibly agitated axe-man is chasing young women in hotpants around the place, everyone instinctively gets what is going on. For instance, every Halloween between 2004 and 2010 saw the release of a new instalment of the horror franchise *Saw*, in which a deranged psychopath called Jigsaw devises a series of murderous games to test the mettle of errant young men and women before dispatching them in increasingly inventive ways. *Saw* had no time for Hollywood stars. All the same, and from humble origins (the first was made for a million dollars, and won high praise at the Sundance Film Festival), it has become the most lucrative horror franchise in film history: the first five in the series made $668 million.

Saw was not to everyone's taste; many critics found its premeditated gore ugly and reprehensible. Just like many HBO shows, it made no attempts to explain itself to a mainstream audience. Instead, its makers had their eye on a global core of avid horror fans. Marketing for the films was kept deliberately cryptic, and made no concessions to the casual viewer. 'If its Halloween,' is all its posters said, 'it must be *Saw*.' Unlike a blockbuster sequel, however, its story arc did not run out of steam. *Saw* was more like a long-running television series than a traditional film, a rolling production in which its horrific story was allowed time to develop. And, just like *The Wire*, it grew to become a powerful niche-buster.

5

On 2 July 2009 one of the most illustrious pillars of journalism, the *Washington Post*, was caught in the act of planning a series of expensive, cosy salons at which lobbyists and executives would be able to schmooze with its writers and each other. The dinners were to be held at the home of the *Post*'s publisher, Katharine Weymouth, price tags of a quarter of a million dollars were mentioned and, in the storm of bad publicity that followed, it seemed that the paper had been reduced to selling access to its reporters for hard cash. Three days later Weymouth published a hand-wringing letter personally apologising to readers for the incident, but it was too late. The newspaper that had made Watergate a byword for political corruption had tripped over its own bauble and ended up knee-deep in Salongate.

That was not the only thing about the story that seemed richly ironic. Salongate was broken by the upstart website and newspaper *Politico*, which had been launched two years previously by a couple of former *Washington Post* staffers. Its editor-in-chief is John Harris, a boyish-looking man in his mid-forties whose career had been spent at the *Post*, where he had risen to become its national political editor. For some years Harris had watched as general-interest newspapers and magazines, facing cutbacks and with so much else to write about, retreated from their coverage of the White House and Capitol Hill. 'Around the year 2005,' he told me, 'reporting began to lose its allure for me and I started to get interested in the larger questions. The more I thought about it, the more I felt that big national newspapers no longer had the advantage. It used to be that the most important thing about a journalist was the designation that came after the name: the *Washington Post* or whatever. That's no longer as true as it was.' Surely, Harris came to believe, in the age of the net there was room for a small news operation that did Washington's political scene and nothing else. Together with his colleague Jim VandeHei and financial backing from a small media company, he thought it would be worth finding out.

In January 2007 *Politico* set up home across the river from Washington in Arlington, Virginia. As if to reinforce the power shift away from big, lumbering general-interest news organisations, it based itself in offices that had once housed the media behemoth Gannett and its paper, *USA Today*. The plan was to start out with twelve reporters, but within a few months that had risen to twenty. It wasn't always easy being the new kid on Washington's block. During a press conference early in the life of the paper, President Bush called on one of its reporters to ask a question and then sniggered that he'd never heard of *Politico*. Before long, however, it was signing up refugees from a host of illustrious news organisations. *Politico* lured Mike Allen away from *Time* magazine, for example, to become chief political correspondent; he went on to break Salongate. As the presidential election of 2008 got under way, it also acquired an enthusiastic new audience of political junkies. By the time the Democratic Party arrived in Denver to anoint Barack Obama as their presidential candidate in August of that year, *Politico* had forty journalists on its payroll and just about all of them were in Denver that day. By the end of 2009 there were seventy-five journalists on the payroll and yearly revenues of twenty million dollars. In only two years it had grown a presence in Washington bigger than any other news organisation.

Politico achieved all this by pumping out a hard-charging, minute-by-minute online diet of what was going on in the White House and on Capitol Hill, and what it meant. Five times a week when Congress is in session, it also distributes a free newspaper within the Washington Beltway; circulation is about thirty-two thousand. Not everyone is enamoured of the new arrival, and its coverage can often seem raspy and overheated. Some critics accuse it of floating insubstantial scoops that melt under closer investigation. Others castigate it for playing 'inside baseball' – of being madly in love with the insular and (to most people) deeply dull goings-on in government bureaucracy. A story about aliens landing in Washington would not likely make the pages of *Politico* unless their leader demanded discussions on interplanetary trade with the president. It did, however, see fit to report on how presidential advisor David M. Axelrod planned to spend his fortieth wedding anniversary. But that, argues Harris, is precisely the point: the paper thrives on the insiderishness of its coverage. 'We don't recoil from that,' he says, 'we embrace it. We're not writing for the average intelligent person in California. People don't come to *Politico* because they have a casual interest in Washington, they come because they have an intense interest, because they're really immersed in this stuff. For those kind of people, we're a must-read.' And because *Politico*'s interests are narrow, it can also afford to go deep: it can step back from day-to-day reporting to mount in-depth investigations. Written for an audience of political geeks, the paper is obsessive about detail, covering legal and budgetary issues in more detail than the average reader could stomach. It can also turn up political scoops. It was *Politico* that first found out about Barack Obama's friendship with the former Weatherman Bill Ayers, and which broke the news that the Republican National Committee had spend one hundred and fifty thousand dollars kitting out Sarah Palin and her family with new clothes.

For journalists on mainstream papers and magazines, *Politico*'s successes must be a little frustrating. Since the nineties, many proprietors had been cutting costs, firing journalists and widening their news remit ever further to hold the attention of their audience. The result was to dilute their ability to offer sustained, authoritative coverage in any particular area. America's most prominent general-interest news magazines, *Time* and *Newsweek*, now operate with less than half the number of Washington staff that they had in the mid-eighties. In the news industry as much as the coffee industry, however, cutting costs and stretching one's product thin was not the only way to go. News magazines that stuck to what they do best have reaped the rewards. By defining its remit very narrowly around its specialist subjects of business, global politics and public policy, *The Economist* has built its reputation for a kind of original journalism its readers would struggle to find anywhere else, and which gives them good reasons to keep coming back. The approach has royally paid off. In the decade to the end of 2009 its circulation almost doubled, from 722,984 copies to 1,420,766. Not only that, but by investing in high-quality reporting and analysis from around the world, *The Economist* has cultivated a genuinely global niche: four-fifths of its readers now come from outside the UK, and over half live in the United States. In the same decade, the story of general-interest weekly news magazines like *Time* and *Newsweek* has been one of steady decline. *Time*'s worldwide circulation fell from 4.07 million in the first half of 2000 to 3.33 million in the second half of 2009, while during the same period *Newsweek*'s circulation fell from 3.14 million to 1.97 million. As news outlets wither, and also lose interest in the minutiae of Washington policy-making, *Politico* is only one of a new breed of niche-busting online newsletters and magazines that have grown up to fill some of the gaps. Most of us will never have heard of any of them, but by February 2009 an obscure one-year-old online newsletter about climate change called *ClimateWire* had ten reporters in Washington – more than Hearst Newspaper Group, which runs sixteen daily papers.

Niche-busters like *Politico* and *ClimateWire* are only seedlings in this new ecosystem, but many of them are showing themselves to be the most fertile sites for original journalism. Not all of them are aimed at business people or technology types, or concerned with the rarefied world of Washington politics. What unites them is that they do not seek to explain things to the general public, but rather to investigate them for audiences whose interests are both narrow and exhaustive. In doing so they are quietly changing the definition of what news is. In virtually no time at all, for example, the LA-based celebrity website TMZ (the name refers to the thirty-mile zone that encloses Hollywood's film and entertainment industry) has set itself up as one of the hottest sources for celebrity news and gossip. News sites like *Politico* and TMZ are unencumbered by the old organisations and ways of doing things, which makes it cheaper and easier for them to concentrate their attention on what they do best. 'Whether it's fly-fishing, sports or Washington politicking,' says John Harris, 'satisfying an intense interest in something means you can have more impact, more efficiently.' Like HBO, they often benefit from disillusion with the mainstream media and wear their upstart credentials on their sleeves. Despite the insiderish way that it reads, *Politico* presents itself as a maverick outsider in Washington. 'The *Washington Post*', the media analyst Michael Wolff told me, 'used to be more powerful than any single person in Washington except the American president. It was a de facto branch of the American government. *Politico*, on the other hand, reports as if it's on the outside, as if it and its readers are gadflies looking in on this strange world, even if that isn't entirely true.' Some of these new niche-busters charge for subscriptions, while others sell their material on to the general-interest papers that don't have the resources to do it themselves. By converting hawkish consumers into regular visitors, many make money from advertisers who dearly want to reach their readers: *Politico* charges a handsome rate to advertisers who want to get their message across to Washington insiders. They can even turn their small but devoted audiences into valuable sources of information. It was thanks to its small army of celebrity-obsessed sources, remember, that on 25 June 2009 TMZ scooped the entire global media with the news that Michael Jackson had just died.

*

In 2007, when *The Sopranos* came to an end, HBO faced a momentary wobble. Chris Albrecht left the company and industry commentators began to wonder aloud whether the channel had 'lost its magic'. It was not, after all, the only home for premium, high-quality drama any more. The cable channel AMC was airing the first series of its highly regarded *Mad Men* (the series had been turned down by HBO) and Showtime was building an enthusiastic audience for its serial-killer show *Dexter*. By focusing all its attention on high-end serial drama, it turned out, HBO had helped to grow the number of places where it could find a home and improved the general diet. 'We showed what was possible to do on television,' Albrecht told a journalist shortly before his departure. 'I think what that did was to bring more people into the category and to spend more money on original scripted programming. It's good for everybody when the bar gets raised.' In the end it was good for HBO too. When its vampire series

True Blood arrived in the autumn of 2008 and proved an unlikely hit, it was clear that the channel had found its feet again. Within a year, it was winning HBO its highest ratings since *The Sopranos*.

The story of HBO suggests that, when everything is thrown into a strange new ecosystem, good things can take a long time to grow. When they do pop up they often do so in unusual new nesting places, and in a colourful array of shapes and sizes. These new nesting places tend to appear on the margins, and to define themselves against the mainstream. Instead of polishing up their brands to attract different audiences, they focus more narrowly and more deeply on producing something distinctive. Then they focus their efforts on serving relatively small groups of enthusiasts. Many of them do not look very kindly on predators that show up occasionally and snack on what is available. Instead they prefer to convert them into regular visitors, or show them the door. To thrive, however, a nesting place needs to grow its audience as well as its stuff. Since many of us identify ourselves by the things we like and the company we keep, the most successful of them foster a sense of belonging, of being apart from the mainstream in a flock of our own. That helps enormously when it comes to persuading us to spread the word.

6

Birds of a Feather

The death of demographics

In which we sort ourselves into flocks

Grant Edwards, a young hog farmer from Bucyrus in Ohio, knows that he owes everything to FarmersOnly.com. Edwards had no trouble finding romantic partners, but they kept grumbling about the long hours he was putting in on the farm, especially when it came to harvest time. Fortunately, that is exactly what Sarah Starkey was looking for. Starkey was not a farmer per se, but she did kept horses, and was a popular barrel-racer at rodeo events. She even lived in nearby Johnstown; both she and Edwards had both attended Ohio State University, but didn't get to know each other there. 'Part of the reason our [past] relationships failed,' Edwards told a local reporter from the *Columbus Dispatch*, 'was that the other person didn't have the same type of background. Agriculture is as much of a lifestyle as it is a job sometimes.' After a brief virtual flirtation, their first date was at a basketball game in February 2006. Eighteen months later they were married, and shortly after the pair moved to a ten-acre farm in nearby Turnbull County to build a life together. In February 2009 came their first child.

Jerry Merrill takes quiet satisfaction from another job well done. 'It's not unusual,' he says. 'I've had a hundred and fifty marriages so far that I know about, and I reckon there's ten times as many that I don't.' A Cleveland ad man in his mid-fifties, Merrill makes an unlikely cupid, planting the seeds of romance among America's farmers. The idea for a dating site came after a conversation with one of his clients, a divorcee who was running her own farm and finding it difficult to meet any suitable men in what little spare time she had. Merrill offered to search around online on her behalf, but came back empty-handed. 'I found hundreds of dating sites which claimed to be right for farmers, but all of them knocked me right back to the big national sites. Even with all their different ways to categorise yourself, you have to spend so much time weeding through all those people to find someone like you.' Deciding to set up a site of his own, Merrill spent six months talking to farmers from all around the country, asking whether they were married and how they went about meeting possible partners. In the end he was amazed that no one appeared to have had the idea before. 'There are a lot of lonely farmers out there,' he says, 'and no wonder. If you walk out your front door in the city you've got ten thousand people within a mile radius and lots of coffee bars and nightclubs. A farmer might have only ten people living within the same radius, and most of those will be taken.' FarmersOnly opened its online doors in May 2005 under the banner 'City folks just don't get it!', and by that October Merrill had nearly two thousand members on his books. Business blossomed when he ran an advert on local television. The ad featured talking animals and the jingle 'You don't have to be lonely, at FarmersOnly', and went on to become a viral hit on YouTube. FarmersOnly now has a hundred thousand members, from all over America and Canada, and the 'barnyard buzz' section of the site has acres of gleeful testimonials. Newcomers are offered a thirty-day trial membership, after which they pay ten dollars a month or sixty dollars a year. Merrill and his son vet each applicant to make sure they fit the profile. 'We spend a lot of time reading through the ads and looking at the pictures. Our motto is clean and green; we don't want vulgar language or people goofing around.' During his research phase Merrill established that farmers tend to marry others in the local community, not necessarily other farmers. This gave rise to a commercial dilemma. 'I wanted it to work not only for farmers, but also for anyone who could relate to the lifestyle. It's really about old-fashioned values.' In the end he chose to define the site narrowly, and the gamble seems to have paid off as he does just as much business among non-farmers who live in small-town or rural areas. 'I've even got some customers in big cities like New York, and they just can't wait to get back into the country.'

FarmersOnly is not for everyone, but that is the point. Living online has made us as highly skilled at hunting out exactly the people we want to reach as the things we want to buy, listen to or read. The life of a hunter-gatherer, however, can be tiring. Whoever coined the adage that there are plenty more fish in the sea could scarcely have imagined colossal dating ecosystems like Match.com in the US and Shaadi.com in India, each of which has tens of millions of members on their books. These catch-all dating agencies give their users plenty of boxes to tick and ways to search, but most try to narrow things down via conventional demographic categories like age, gender, sexuality and location – and even after all that there is usually an enormous pool of potential partners to sift through. Perhaps as a result, they have been losing ground to special-interest competitors. Between 2005 and 2009, according to statistics from Hitwise, the number of dating sites on the web rose from 916 to 1430, with the biggest growth among those cultivating a niche; 44 per cent of them were niche outfits, according to industry-watchers at Online Personals Watch, up from 35 per cent in 2006. Thrown into an ocean of potential matches and forced to fend for ourselves, it seems, many of us would prefer it if there were fewer fish in the sea.

Specialist agencies now exist for just about every ethnic group and religious denomination, but most new arrivals prefer to zero in on shared interests. Incarcerated lonely hearts and their admirers can go to Womenbehindbars.com, animal-lovers to Lovemelovemypets.com, music lovers to Asoundmatch.com and horsey types to Equestriansingles.com, while the rich or greedy can make for MillionaireMatch.com. Like FarmersOnly, many of them define themselves against the mainstream. 'Geeks are special', newcomers to the dating agency Geek 2 Geek are advised in a welcome message. 'Their interests just aren't the same as most people's. As a result, traditional dating sites just don't work well for them.' Most of the new arrivals work hard to maintain quality control. In January 2010, it was revealed that the niche dating site BeautifulPeople.com ('the largest network of attractive people in the world') had sent five thousand members packing after complaints that they had gained weight over the holiday period. When reporters asked the reason for the cull, the site's founder Robert Hintze explained that 'letting fatties roam the site is a direct threat to our business model'.

That many of us are seeking out love online in specialist stores rather than supermarkets is hardly surprising. The bigger the online ecosystem we find ourselves in, the more we want to huddle together in groups. But what kind of groups? Released into an almost limitless environment, it seems, we are heading straight for roosts that tightly define themselves around the things we really like. It is easy to see why. Gathering around stuff that we're passionate about and sharing it around makes it easier to deepen our appreciation and forage for more of it. It also makes the online universe more manageable. A shared passion for farming, for example, can help us avoid being floored by an ocean wave of potential partners on online dating sites; it gives us something to talk about, helps us find people we like as well as things we enjoy. By sorting ourselves into groups based on these things we are gradually defying the attributes and the groups chosen for us by the big beasts and replacing them with those chosen by ourselves. In short, we are exhibiting the nesting and flocking behaviour of migratory birds.

2

One evening in 1995, a teacher called Maria Sebregondi was at home reading a book. She found herself returning to the same three paragraphs again and again. Sebregondi was from Rome, where she taught literature and poetry, and brought up her children. Her real passion, however, was for building stories around beautiful objects, and the previous year she had begun to help out at a small Milanese company. Modo & Modo called itself a publisher but it didn't really produce anything of its own. Instead it traded in the kind of bohemian ephemera – cute translucent gadgets, pens colourful enough to whet the appetite of stationery fetishists, T-shirts printed with quotes from famous philosophers – that only finds a market where students and design enthusiasts are present in large concentrations. If Modo & Modo was to grow it needed to start making its own stuff, which is why its founder Francesco Franceschi had hired Maria Sebregondi to come up with a few ideas.

Sebregondi is a slightly built woman whose delicate clothes and rimless glasses seem judged to fit perfectly; when I met her in her office, the only thing on the table was a copy of *Artforum* magazine. The book she had been reading that night in 1995 was *The Songlines*, by the English travel writer Bruce Chatwin, and the paragraphs hindering her progress were those in which the author laments the disappearance of the distinctive hardcover notebooks, bound in oilcloth, that he purchased in Paris and did most of his writing in. These notebooks were called moleskines, and each time Chatwin returned to Paris he would pick up a fresh supply from his favourite stationer. 'The pages were squared and the end-papers held in place with an elastic band,' he writes in *The Songlines*. 'I had numbered them in series. I wrote my name and address on the front page, offering a reward to the finder. To lose a passport was the least of one's worries: to lose a notebook was a catastrophe.' Now, however, the proprietor of the shop was informing him that they were becoming more and more difficult to get hold of. '"I'd like to order a hundred," I said to Madame. "A hundred will last me a lifetime." She promised to telephone Tours at once, that afternoon . . . At five, I kept my appointment with Madame. The manufacturer had died. His heirs had sold the business. She removed her spectacles and, almost with an air of mourning, said, "*Le vrai moleskine n'est plus.*"'

The story of the moleskines' departure from the world moved Sebregondi greatly. 'I'd been a student in Paris in the eighties,' she told me, 'and I well remembered writing in exactly those same diaries. I still have many of them at home.' By making a few enquiries, Sebregondi was able to confirm that the firm in Tours was indeed the last manufacturer of moleskine notebooks, and that it had stopped making them in 1986 after the death of its owner. *The Songlines* was published in 1987, and Chatwin himself died only two years later. He was not the only noteworthy moleskine devotee. With a little more research Sebregondi was able to discover that a great many artists and writers associated with the twentieth-century avant-garde had used the same kind of notebook to draw or write down their first drafts. In 1995 a Matisse exhibition had arrived in Rome and Sebregondi couldn't help noticing that his sketchbooks bore striking similarities to the moleskine notebooks she was used to. Then she'd visited the Picasso museum in Paris and saw that many of the little black books which housed Picasso's sketches – their size, their pockets, their distinctive elastic bands – looked very much like moleskines. So, on closer inspection, did the journals of Ernest Hemingway and André Breton. It was as if the whole history of the avant-garde had revolved around a single hard-cover notebook held together by an elastic band. 'Here was a story steeped in culture,' says Sebregondi, 'rich in imagination and tied to a grand historical tradition. So why not bring it back to life?' When she put her idea to Francesco Franceschi and brought in one of her old notebooks to show him ('Here's a better story than those boring T-shirts,' is how she remembers her argument) he was impressed. Together they set about trying to make it work.

A year later, in 1996, Sebregondi moved up to Milan and began working more closely on the project. In that year, too, Modo & Modo trademarked their brand as Moleskine (with a capital 'M') and located a manufacturer in China capable of assembling notebooks to their detailed design specification. The first Moleskine notebooks arrived from China to be hand-finished in Milan in 1997: that year Modo & Modo sold five thousand of them to their Italian distributors, and the following year it shifted thirty thousand. In 1999 the company expanded into its European neighbours, and sales began an exponential ascent. By 2003 they had reached three million a year, two years later they were at 4.5 million, and in August 2006 the company was bought by a French investment fund for €60 million. Since then, growth has continued unabated. The company sells around ten million notebooks a year, and Americans buy more of them than anyone else. Moleskines can be found in up-market gift shops, stationers and booksellers in sixty-one different countries. At the ICA they took pride of place in the bookshop. The company has also diversified its range. As well as notebooks it now produces diaries, city guides and lavishly produced limited editions, many of which riff on the distinguished history of the product. 'The legendary notebook of Hemingway, Picasso and Chatwin', a note in the inside pocket informs each buyer, which is not quite the whole truth. 'It's an exaggeration,' Francesco Franceschi told the *New York Times* in 2004. 'It's marketing, not science. It's not the absolute truth.' It might even be a fitting epitaph for the moles of the avant-garde to find themselves preserved within plastic film in an item of stationery that only has a glancing acquaintance with their radical past. 'No mole has been disturbed to make our notebooks,' Sebregondi giggles, and she's perfectly right.

Maria Sebregondi's genius was to turn the memory of the avant-garde into a handsome product that people could identify with. A good deal of Moleskine's success, she believes, has been fuelled by low-cost airlines and the arrival of nomadic, culture-loving types who want an attractive writing accessory to take with them on their travels. But it goes deeper than that, she believes. 'In the nineteenth and twentieth centuries, people took their identities from their home and their place of work. It was all very static. Now identity is more likely to be bound up with memory and culture, and with the things people can take with them – their notebook, their mobile phone, their Facebook page and their followers on Twitter. That's their place.' It nonetheless took the energetic evangelism of Moleskine's fans to help them find it.

Starting around the year 2002, Sebregondi remembers becoming aware of a flurry of online chatter puffing up her notebooks. 'There were all these different groups of people talking excitedly about it, and the odd thing was that many of them were young people working with computers and information technology. It was as if they were rediscovering the pleasure of direct experience, of going around writing things down by hand.' It all seems to have started with a lecturer at MIT, who took to mentioning how useful he found the notebooks in his lectures and in his university blog. Not long after that it turned up on a website associated with GTD (Getting Things Done), a time-management craze popular among IT workers. Soon websites were springing up specifically to further appreciation of the Moleskine. One of the most popular is called Moleskinerie.com, and it owes its origins to a Chicago-based photographer called Armand Frasco. Frasco booked the domain name for Moleskinerie on a whim in January 2004 after a cursory Google search revealed lots of others who were just as mad about Moleskines as he was. In a single afternoon he read through the online conversation and invited everyone he could find to his new site. Many of them took him up on his offer: within weeks Moleskinerie was attracting five thousand visitors a day, and Frasco was spending much of his day maintaining it. A year later Francesco Franceschi called and offered him some help, and since then he's been working closely with the company. 'Two kinds of people who come here,' Frasco told me. 'There are newbies who've bought a Moleskine on impulse and who want to know more about it and what they can use it for, and then there are hardcore enthusiasts who want to know everything – which notebooks are the sturdiest, which are the best for sketching in, how the virgin paper is made and which fountain pens respond to it best.' For Moleskine, the relationship offers a valuable opportunity to listen to the views of its most zealous followers. 'We're like an informal focus group, and that's a big advantage for them,' says Frasco. 'They're able to visit the site and glean knowledge and suggestions from everyone's comments.'

Moleskinerie is no longer the only site available to Moleskine enthusiasts. Chinese fans have set up Moleskiner.cn while Russians can go to Moleskinerie.ru; fan sites are mushrooming everywhere the notebooks are sold, from Brazil to the Philippines. Then there are the dozens of blogs and over fifty Facebook groups, all dedicated to the love of Moleskine. Frasco himself inaugurated the first group on the photo-sharing site Flickr, so that his users could display pictures of their Moleskines and their sketches. It has fourteen thousand members, and is now only one of many Moleskine-themed groups on the site. 'There are a huge number of groups of fans out there using our notebooks, and all of it happened very spontaneously,' confirms Maria Sebregondi. The first time she went to Shanghai, she emailed the owner of Moleskiner.cn and asked to meet him. 'I had no idea who he was, but he turned out to be really nice.'

In less than a decade, Moleskine notebooks have been resurrected and turned into the totem of a vibrant global subculture. Much of it is down to the internet as fan sites, most of them operating entirely independently of the company, do most of its marketing for free. In chapter 3 we saw how, since the sixties, moles have been burrowing beneath mainstream culture. Before long there was a rich and varied network of subcultures underground – punks and rockers, hippies and casuals – all of which identified themselves by the way they dressed and behaved, and by their hostility to mainstream culture. Now they have all faded, of course, but as mainstream culture crumbles and we spend more time online, exotic and wildly diverse new boltholes are opening up, from Moleskinerie.com to FarmersOnly.com. These new internet subcultures bring together small groups of people from different parts of the world around the things they happen to really like. Their members do not need distinctive dress codes to identify themselves to each other because they can easily find each other via the net. Most of them do not want to throw stones at or overthrow the mainstream, but simply to band together in a club of their own.

Not everyone is impressed. Mocking the creative pretensions of Moleskine enthusiasts, the satirical website Stuff White People Like (motto: 'they pretend to be unique, yet somehow they're all exactly the same') suggests that 'when you see a white person with one of these notebooks, you should always ask them about what sort of projects they are working on in their free time. But you should never ask to actually see the notebook lest you ask the question "how are you going to make a novel out of five phone numbers and a grocery list?"' But maybe the conversation is part of the point. Remember that time you passed a stranger reading a book you love, and idly contemplated striking up a conversation about it? On the internet you can. The net is such a massive expanse that when we stumble upon something it is easy to think of it as a part of ourselves. Bunching into subcultures reinforces that sense of specialness, and gives fans a supportive environment in which they can express their shared identification and find out more. What they offer is a nesting place, and a flock to fly with.

3

How does a novice progress to become a fan? Over eighteen months an Argentinian sociologist called Claudio Benzecry tried to find out. He attended seventy performances at the Teatro Colón opera house in his native Buenos Aires, sometimes returning to see the same opera six times, and took bus trips to other opera houses hundreds of miles away. He also talked to those beside him in the audience. In his subsequent paper 'Becoming a Fan: On the Seductions of Opera', published in 2009, he reports a typical scene while he and his fellow opera-goers wait in the queue to get in:

> The flyers immediately become a catalyst for conversation among strangers. I am standing next to a woman in her early sixties who looks briefly at the flyer before exclaiming, 'I heard the first night was a disaster.'

> She adjusts her large glasses and goes on, 'I haven't gone yet, but my girlfriend went and said it was a mess. I'm going on Sunday. Have you gone already?' Before I can reply, the woman is rhapsodizing about how good 'she' was the first time she saw the same opera at the Colón. Soon, our conversation is joined by the older gentleman in front of the woman and the young man behind me. It seems that everyone knows who 'she' is but me. Before I can embarrass myself by asking, the older gentleman says, 'But La Piscitelli was extraordinary. It's hardly a surprise, if you consider how good she has been before.' Before I can say something about how I remembered her in Norma, the three of them start exchanging notes. 'I think that what she did in *Simon* [*Boccanegra*] was amazing,' says the young man, to which the older man responds, 'Yes, but I thought she fared even better the time she went toe to toe with June Anderson as Norma!'

Even if we have never been to the opera, most of us will have overheard a conversation just like this. Many of those interviewed by Claudio Benzecry had too. The majority had been introduced to opera by chance: one happened to hear it on the radio, while another came across it in the course of her romance with an amateur musician. For most it was love at first sight. Fans described the 'intense' and 'explosive' nature of the attraction on their first encounter. One said that the music 'vibrated at the same frequency' as her body while another believed that it 'pounded in time with the rhythm of her heart'. On its own, though, it was not enough to make them fanatics. For that, something else was required, and Benzecry found it in the audience. The opera-goers he spoke to understood that opera has to be learned if it is to be fully appreciated. To get to grips with it they went to see as many operas as they could, but they did other things too: they attended meetings and conferences, bought records and related books, and generally found out more about it. To point them in the right direction they relied on more experienced fans. What Benzecry discovered was an 'informal apprenticeship process in which the older members school the younger ones and are recognized and revered for their knowledge'. Novices grew to value the opera not only by watching it, in other words, but by learning about it from others more knowledgeable than themselves. This informal schooling took place on bus trips, during intermissions, in the queue at the opera house door. It even happened during the opera itself. Novices clapped too often and at the wrong times, which tended to give them away. 'The immediate response is generally an exasperated "Shhh!"' recorded the sociologist, 'that is often even louder than the clapping.'

Opera is high culture, but it is hardly unique. The path from novice to connoisseur, Claudio Benzecry's work suggests, is about learning to value something more, and it is often eased by enthusiasts around us, in the audience and in the places where we meet them. Increasingly, those places are online. While he laments the retreat of the mainstream media from opera coverage, the classical music critic Alex Ross points to a new kind of compact emerging among critics, professional musicians and fans online: 'What's grown up,' he told me, 'is a much greater diversity of voices, a vital conversation.' Opera buffs are not the only ones who have been flocking together under cover of the net. So too are Beanie Baby enthusiasts. Beanie Babies are a series of furry, fist-sized soft toys that for a time were produced only in small batches. Soon after eBay's launch in 1995, there began a full-scale run on Beanie Babies; in May 1997 alone the site sold half a million dollars' worth of them, and eBay made the decision to hand them their own retail category. They were also fetching excellent prices: a Beanie Baby that had retailed for five dollars was now going for an average of thirty-three dollars. The simplest explanation was that Beanie Babies were only made available in limited editions, which made them seem very distinctive purchases. Since the internet excels in its ability to bring together buyers and sellers from far and wide, markets for distinctive items tend to become thicker with potential buyers, which often drives prices up. But that was not the only reason for the hike. Beanie Baby collectors gathered from all over America to collect their favourite toys on eBay; the site gave them the opportunity to find each other as well as the toys themselves. 'Collectors are people with a passion,' says Adam Cohen in his biography of eBay, *The Perfect Store*, 'and they seek out others who share their passion. Before the internet, many collectors were geographically isolated. Someone in a small town with an interest in Depression glass or Southern folk art might have trouble finding like-minded people nearby. But on the internet, thousands of collectors with the same fascination were only a few mouse-clicks away.' By bringing them together in one virtual place, eBay allowed Beanie Baby enthusiasts to deepen their appreciation of the toys and find out more about them, which made them even more valuable.

To Dan Ariely, a professor of behavioural economics at the Massachusetts Institute of Technology, none of this is very surprising. As we are initiated into a group of enthusiasts for anything, we become better at distinguishing nuances, which only makes the activity even more pleasurable. Think about bird watching, he says. 'The further you get into a group of bird watchers, chatting about different birds and who's seen what, the more interesting everything seems.' But there is something else going on too, he believes. Once inside these groups the behaviour we exhibit is often deeply tribal, especially those which have grown up on the net. 'In hunter-gatherer society, it used to be that when you killed an animal you'd wear its skin to show it was you who'd killed it. Then we had expensive cars and clothes as a way of expressing ourselves to others. Now places like Facebook and Twitter give us whole new tools to communicate who we are to those we like. And after a while, a common language develops about what's valuable and what's not.' Ariely likes the example of Farmville, a game played on Facebook that invites people to grow and manage their own virtual farms. By 2010 Farmville had collected nearly twenty-two million fans; there's likely to be some overlap in its membership with FarmersOnly.com. But why would anyone bother to build a virtual farm? 'It's because others in our online group can come and appreciate it, and we can say, "Hey look at my farm and all my beautiful animals." It's a way for people to enhance their prestige and their social currency within the group.'

In the right hands, social currency can morph into real currency. Google's Hal Varian told me the story of a friend of his son's, who had taken a job in a Japanese company with an unusual approach to retailing. The idea came about when someone noticed that the kind of clothes worn by young people in trendy Tokyo districts like Roppongi looked very much like the stuff that was turning up in American charity shops. 'These were very distinctive garments, and they were assembled with great care. This week it might be bowling shirts, next week it might be paisley ties or chequered scarves. So the company paid some spotters to go out in those neighbourhoods and take a close look at their outfits, take photos and then email those photos off to the United States. At the other end, they had several hundred people travel around second-hand or charity shops in little American towns and pick out similar clothes. They were immediately flown to Tokyo, dry-cleaned and were available in Tokyo shops within a few days.' That clothes coveted by Japanese youth came to be plundered from American charity shops was not only because the internet's global reach drove up prices for distinctive gear. It was also because of the rumblings of the teenage subculture in which they played so integral a part. 'If you were the latest to get hold of one of these cool items of apparel,' says Varian, 'that raised your standing within the group.'

Opera-goers, teenage subcultures and Beanie Baby enthusiasts aren't the only ones who learn to appreciate things as part of a group. 'What happens in a book club?' asks Hal Varian, before answering his own rhetorical question. 'You all read a book and discuss it, but presumably what's valuable is the discussion itself.' It's an instructive example, because the environment for book clubs has changed utterly in recent years. Membership of the general-interest Book-of-the-Month Club has been leaking away for decades. Just like the high-street book chains, the company responded by diluting its literary fare in an attempt to scoop its audience back up. The problem with that approach was that hawkish customers could easily pick up a copy of the latest John Grisham or Tom Clancy thriller from Amazon or their local supermarket, and at a heftier discount than the Book-of-the-Month Club could manage. In 2000, following a corporate merger, the Book-of-the-Month Club was brought within a bigger book club umbrella called Bookspan.

Bookspan immediately set about establishing new specialist book clubs under a range of different reading themes like Christian, new-age, mystery, craft and business. Interest in the Book-of-the-Month Club, meanwhile, continued to dwindle. By 2004 its membership stood at seven hundred thousand, less than half of the number it was able to muster in its heyday. In the same year, in an effort to catch up with its readers, it announced plans to divide its monthly recommendation into six different categories, including mystery and self-help. It didn't work. Only two years later, in 2006, membership had halved again to 345,000, and the Book-of-the-Month Club had been overtaken by Black Expressions, Bookspan's African-American themed club which had accumulated 460,000 members in just seven years.

Bookspan now has about five million members marshalled in over twenty different clubs, but the Book-of-the-Month Club amounts to only a tiny fraction of them. Readers do not seem to be able to identify with it. Thrown into a new publishing ecosystem, they have migrated to clubs that match their particular interests. It is not difficult to work out why. 'With the internet you can have a book club of just about any size,' says Hal Varian, 'but too large and it becomes unmanageable. In a shared group with your friends or people who share a common interest, on the other hand, it's going to be much more focused.' Like niche dating agencies, niche book clubs cultivate common interests in anything from science fiction to religion to a shared political outlook. Whereas The Book-of-the-Month Club was only a club in name – its members never really met – many of these new arrivals bring their members together, either face to face or online. Just as Varian says, their value seems to lie less in discounts than in discussion. Talking to each other helps readers refine their appreciation of the books and authors that they love, and to find out more. As much as opera-goers, it sets them on a path to becoming fully fledged fans.

4

Become an enthusiast for something and you are more likely to want to pass it on. Barack Obama knows this more than anyone. By the time he stood up in a Denver football stadium to accept the Democratic Party's nomination for the presidency on 28 August 2008 there were eighty-four thousand ecstatic fans in the audience. The choice of venue was appropriate, because the atmosphere was more akin to a sporting event than a political rally. The decision to open up the event to the public as well as Party delegates was deliberate too. 'We were a grass-roots campaign,' writes Obama's campaign manager David Plouffe in his memoir, *The Audacity to Win*, 'and it felt wrong that our biggest night so far could not be shared with those who had selflessly given so much time and effort.' That was not the only reason to have them there. No sooner had they arrived in the stadium than Obama fans were being urged to call or send text messages to their friends and family asking them to watch the speech. They were also invited to use onc of 130 telephones dotted around the stadium to tell unregistered voters about the campaign and ask them for their mobile number or email address.

Denver was only the icing on the cake. At around the same time, Plouffe was emailing the millions of Obama fans who had registered with the campaign website, asking for a donation of twenty-five dollars or more. Around the country supporters had got together to organise nearly five thousand parties to coincide with the acceptance speech, and many of those who turned up to them were chivvied into making calls and sending texts. Rather than mere supporters, Obama's team wanted enthusiasts, whose primary responsibility was to spread the word.

Thomas Gensemer was in Denver that evening, and well remembers the excitement of it all. Eighteen months earlier the shaven-headed young dotcom entrepreneur and his firm Blue State Digital had been given the task of revving up Obama's campaign with the internet and new media. The call from David Plouffe came two weeks before the announcement of Obama's candidacy in February 2007. Three years later, when I met him, he still seemed in awe of the experience. 'They said, "It's clear that this is going to be at the centre of our campaign. How quickly can we get something going?"' What Gensemer and his team came up with was a website called MyBarackObama.com, and they were still tweaking it an hour before the official announcement address. It has often been compared to Facebook, but Gensemer is healthily sceptical of those who put too much of their faith in shiny new objects like Facebook and Twitter. The point of MyBarackObama, he says, was not just to get people to click a button or chat to each other online, but to inspire them to donate money, organise house parties and knock on doors. 'The goal was always to put someone to work. If you signed up in a certain state, our goal was to get you connected as soon as possible to another volunteer or campaign office. It was about asking for donations, about bringing your friends to the rally, about texting five people to get them involved. The best representation of your valuing this relationship was your decision to bring someone to the party.'

The army of volunteers was soon growing nicely. Within a month MyBarackObama.com had 450,000 online sign-ups, many them driven there by public meetings, and donations from those who had signed up were rolling in at a phenomenal rate. Not long after that, having everyone pull out their mobile and call or text five of their friends became standard operating procedure at Obama rallies. 'It was remarkable organic growth,' writes David Plouffe in his memoir, 'that revealed a core of passionate early devotees.' Thanks to the website, Obama's team often had a campaigning presence in a state even before the first Obama staffer touched down. It also proved useful as a means of putting existing members in touch with other, so as to reinforce their identification with the campaign. One such scheme was known as 'Grassroots match'. 'Say that you gave ten bucks,' says Gensemer. 'We would say we're going to introduce you to ten others and you're going to challenge each other to give another ten bucks. Doing that helped you put a name and a face to people around the country who were aligned in the same purpose.' It seemed to work. By the time of Obama's acceptance speech his campaign had two million campaign contributors, almost all of whom were volunteers.

It would be difficult to overstate how far Barack Obama's campaign bypassed the traditional machinery of the Democratic Party. In the early months of 2007 he was a rank outsider without access to either media or resources, or even much in the way of organisation. In *The Audacity to Win*, David Plouffe likens it to a start-up business, pitted against Hilary Clinton's organisational goliath. 'She was the eight-hundred-pound gorilla with organisations in every state, 100 per cent name recognition, and a fundraising machine ready to be switched on at a moment's notice. We had none of this. Nothing, nada, zilch.' But even as the campaign gathered momentum and Democratic Party stalwarts offered to help, Plouffe's book makes clear, Obama's team reached over their heads and used their legions of volunteers to make a direct appeal to voters. Underlying all this was the disintegration of the political mainstream.

Even before Richard Nixon's famous television address in 1969, in which he identified a silent majority of Americans who wanted no truck with the counter-culture and were uncomfortable with the ructions over civil rights, both parties had done their best to water down their campaign messages so they could be filtered through the mainstream media. Hillary Clinton's campaign was steeped in that tradition; she bent over backwards in her determination to appeal to middle America and paid the utmost attention to how the contest was playing out on broadcast television. The middle ground of American political life, however, is not what it used to be. Obama's team spent much of their time going around it. When ABC News broke the story of his friendship with the militant pastor Jeremiah Wright, for example, Obama's response – his famous speech on race – was delivered on a Tuesday morning, when most people were at work. It didn't matter, because tens of millions of people watched the speech on YouTube. Hillary Clinton also came armed with the pollster Mark Penn. It was Mark Penn who pioneered the art of using demographic data to slice up the electorate into myriad constituencies in the mid nineties. As the technology improved and data about our shopping habits was added, the technique had been refined into something called 'micro-targeting', enabling pollsters to home in on ever-smaller groups of voters to work out how they might vote. By the time of Obama's bid, however, micro-targeting had lost its touch. Early on in the campaign, David

Plouffe remembers that he and his team 'thought this was an election with one big macrotrend – change – and thought Penn's penchant for slicing and dicing the electorate could come back to bite them'. In the end, that is exactly what happened. The tiny micro-constituencies identified by pollsters seemed to crumble as soon as they were built, leaving Penn and his polling data high and dry. After watching one rousing Obama rally, Penn was heard to remark that his supporters 'look like Facebook'.

None of this is to say that Obama's team did not have very precise information at its fingertips. In fact, Thomas Gensemer is at his most excited when talking about how to harvest voters and their data. It was his firm that spent five million dollars of Obama's campaign contributions on Google search keywords. It was a Blue State Digital staffer, too, who'd dreamed up the 'be the first to know' initiative – the idea that, five days before Obama's acceptance speech, the news that Joe Biden was to be his running mate should be shared first with anyone who'd registered their mobile number with the campaign. When I asked him why he didn't make more use of Facebook, Gensemer laughed. 'If I give Facebook all the data, I don't have it. The reason for MyBarackObama.com wasn't to build an application like Facebook but to provide tools through which we could collect data and know more about you.' One reading of Barack Obama's campaign, in fact, is that it was a data-gathering exercise of unprecedented proportions. Trained volunteers would log in to MyBarackObama.com, where they would be assigned twenty-five telephone numbers to call in their local area. 'And all the while they'd be collecting data and clicking it into the website from home – are you likely to vote, what issues are you most concerned about? That allowed us to target our efforts. It meant we know when to hit you and how to talk to you better.' His team also made a note of whether and when people opened emails from the campaign and which issues they responded to. 'It's amazing how much you can learn about one's response to email,' says Gensemer. Just like the other candidates, his team had voter lists and shopping data at their disposal as the campaign progressed, but they proved much less useful than the information coming in from the volunteers themselves. 'It's helpful to have that stuff in the background, but it's much more useful when people respond to emails voluntarily. With enough grassroots energy, the data begins to grow itself and come in from everywhere. Then it's more about managing it than collecting it.' Based on all the information flowing in, Gensemer was able to divide everyone his volunteers came across into five hundred different groups. 'If I knew that you were with us from the day that Barack announced his candidacy, I'd have people speak to you differently. It's a mixture of how long we've known you, how you've responded, the number of friends you've referred.'

Despite all his data-gathering, Thomas Gensemer is adamant that the politics of the campaign were overarching and never negotiable. 'At its heart was a message about change together with an outsider ethic. We controlled the narrative.' Having a message inspiring enough for people to identify with was nonetheless enormously helpful in getting it around. By the time of Barack Obama's victory over John McCain in November 2008, Gensemer and his team had raised $560 million from 3.2 million donors. They had the email addresses of 13.5 million people on their database, more than half of whom had been recruited by friends involved in the campaign. Instead of heading for the middle ground or going after groups of voters one at a time, Obama's team won by cultivating a modest but energetic clump of enthusiasts – a kind of subculture. As this flock of Obama fans grew they were more than happy to share their information with each other and the campaign. The goal in collecting their data wasn't to dilute the message or to tailor it for different audiences, but to keep people passing it on to anyone who might be interested. In less than two years it had expanded to thirteen million Americans, a fifth of the number who ended up voting for Obama.

5

Barack Obama's campaign for the presidency was out of the ordinary. It came with a distinctive message about change and renewal, which helped it echo around the country and inspire a great many people. But that was not the only thing unusual about it. For some time, political parties have been using information about us – how old we are and our gender, our ethnicity, our sexual preferences and where we live – to help them predict how we might vote. Most of it was guesswork: reading between the lines of datasets and asking questions of small samples of the population in the hope of extrapolating more general significance. Obama's campaign team did something fresh. They cultivated a small core of fans who readily forwarded information about themselves and others they spoke to on the campaign's behalf. They ended up with a trove of information about real people, defined not by their demographic attributes but by how much they identified themselves with Obama, which issues they were most interested in, who they knew who was already involved and how likely they were to vote for him.

To pollsters and questionnaire sociologists, this is a novel way of working. Instead of identifying people via their accidental characteristics, it identifies them by the things they are interested in. It's catching on. While we amble around online, teams of ethnographic bird watchers are observing us to see who we're flocking with and what we are tweeting about. One of them is a woman called Margaret Francis and, when I visited her in her office in San Francisco, she gave me a crash course in how to do it. In her previous career Francis spent much of her time separating customers into different demographic groups, but when I asked her about it she rolled her eyes as if it were ancient history. Francis is employed by a company called Scout Labs, and she and her colleagues have trained a computer programme that can recognise thousands of words which come up in publicly accessible online conversation. She does not need to know anything about the people she is eavesdropping on; she doesn't even need to know their names. The only thing she cares about is what they are saying about her clients. What comes out the other end, she showed me, is a bar chart tracking the murmurings of online opinion about different companies. It is not as easy as it sounds. Recognising the nuances of online conversation can be a tricky business, and Francis has one of her analysts read through the data to look for discrepancies and make sure the computer is getting it right. 'We had motherfucker on the list as a negative word,' she told me, 'and then we were like "why does the machine think this is negative and a person thinks this it's positive?" And then you look at the content, and it says "badass motherfucker" – and motherfucker is only a bad word, it turns out, if it isn't preceded by "badass" or "that righteous". There are all these permutations of motherfucker that are good.'

Most of us cannot get excited enough about products to want to enthuse about them online. On the other hand, we are very keen to identify ourselves with the things we really like. Everywhere from FarmersOnly.com to Moleskinerie.com, we are developing passionate attachments to the most recherché of interests and flocking together with those who feel the same way. The people we join up with online are not usually our friends, but those with whom we share a passion or an affinity. Music is a good example. 'Fashion, subcultures and nightlife all emerge through music,' note the academics Danah Boyd and Irina Shklovski in their 2006 article 'Bands and Fans'. 'When fans "friend" bands [on sites like MySpace], they want to publicly display their fandom . . . by explicitly featuring connection to their favourite bands, fans use music to express who they are.' Identify with something, however, and it is easier for other people to identify you with it too. As we are grazing, companies are tracking our trail and building a very sophisticated picture of our interests. But just as it is hard work hunting out everything we are after on our own, which is why we get together in flocks, companies don't usually have the time or the energy to go after us one by one. Sorting us into groups based on the things we really like allows them to stand back from what we are consuming at any one time to take a broader view of who we are. If they are lucky, like Barack Obama or Beanie Babies, we are already doing it for them. But even if we are not, the ways we identify ourselves online can help them predict other things we might like.

In 2009, an enterprising computer science academic at the University of Texas called Murat Kantarcioglu used his Facebook account to download the information posted on 167,000 Facebook profiles and the three million friendship links between them. Together with one of his research students he wanted to see if they could work out people's politics on the basis of what they liked and who they knew. The pair started with the interests and allegiances of those who had explicitly mentioned whether they were Democrats or Republicans, and then worked backwards to see how far they could use them to predict the politics of everyone else. Everything went through the computer, Kantarcioglu told me. If someone was a fan of an adventure film called *End of the Spear*, they were much more likely to vote Republican. If they were fans of Amnesty International or a member of a Facebook group called 'Every time I see a cute Republican boy, something inside me dies', they were ticked off as probable Democrats. By removing the political affiliations listed by another sample they were able to test their handiwork. Four times out of five, they were right – people's interests, passions and affiliations served as an accurate guide to their voting behaviour.

The research student who worked with Kantarcioglu on the politics prediction project has since gone on to work for Facebook. Other students of his have found jobs with eBay and Cisco. The internet giants and mobile phone companies who have invited us into their online ecosystems have vast amounts of information about us at their disposal, and they are looking for analysts to help them make use of it. These new trend-spotters and cool-hunters are better at recognising algorithms than Adidas, but they are more effective than their predecessors. They don't need to hang out with teenagers to find out what's hip because they can read it from their profiles online; they don't need to know where the trend-setters are because they can see from the dots on their screen who's out clubbing and how they are clustering around retail areas the day after.

Since their subjects are anonymous cookies on a computer screen or dots on a map, much of what they do bypasses conventional demographic methods of identifying who we are. After a while, though, they are able to detect patterns in our electronic movements, which they use to divide us into flocks and predict what we might want to do next. One of them is Cisco's Dan Scheinman and, when I asked him whether there isn't something sinister about it, he told me a story. He used to live in Beijing in the mid-eighties, he said, when the communications infrastructure was antiquated and information was not freely available. Lots of interesting things were happening in the city, however, and somehow everyone got to know what was going on. It was as if something primitive and tribal had taken over, passing information from person to person without anyone even noticing. 'And all we're doing,' he argues, 'is to replicate that with data and make it useful.' Putting people together in groups according to their demographic characteristics, according to Scheinman, was nothing more than 'voodoo science' – it served a purpose when we didn't have anything better, but now it is laughably old-fashioned. What is replacing it, he believes, are allegiances forged around the films, books and music that we really enjoy. For all the hullabaloo about our friends on Facebook and our followers on Twitter, Scheinman believes that they are far from infallible guides to what we want. 'Content is the tribal identifier of the twenty-first century,' he says. 'I happen to listen to the music of sixteen-year-olds; I'm not proud of it but I still do it. I might behave more like a sixteen-year-old girl from Melbourne than any of my Facebook friends. Our interests bring us together, even if we don't know it. And we should be able to bring all that to you.'

With his thicket of gingery hair and his gently protruding paunch, Scheinman doesn't look much like a sixteen-year-old girl. He doesn't talk like one either. Within three minutes of inviting me into a Cisco meeting room he was up at a whiteboard, working furiously with a green felt-tip to illustrate how the big beasts of the music industry have tripped over themselves again and again trying to respond to their new online environment. When I interrupted him to query something he muttered 'Bullshit' and kept on writing. There are advantages to be had, Scheinman believes, in our willingness to congregate around the stuff that we really like. The best way to make up the shortfall in music-buying, for example, is to focus on a small core of enthusiasts and make them a more distinctive offer. 'It's the stuff around the product that they really want – the short clips, the background, the merchandise, the chat with the author, the photos of a live gig.' Put it all in the same place online, he says, and the most enthusiastic fans will come to find it. He opens his laptop and shows me a website he's just built for a Tennessee rock band called Paramore. It's an aggregation of their entire digital existence, he says – twitter feeds, photos from their mobile phones, behind-the-scenes nerves from when one of them was preparing to go on to *The Tonight Show*. 'All this stuff is highly distinctive and very difficult to find anywhere else. If someone buys a subscription to a fan club for thirty dollars a year to get better tickets, for example, that all mounts up. You start with the small stuff to get going, and over time it grows and raises its value.' There are other benefits too. By forging a closer relationship with their biggest fans, artists and performers will be able to make better decisions and justify more original work. 'When you don't really know your audience, you just find the most elementary things they have in common. It's led us to us being a culturally less rich place,' he explains. And then, suddenly, he becomes almost emotional. 'And honestly this is what I hope. What demographics and Nielsen [the company that measures the size and make-up of audiences for the mainstream media] have led us to is the lowest common denominator. As we get to know niche audiences, we'll realise that there's an under-served market for quality stuff.'

It is a good argument, and one whose implications go far beyond the music industry. As everyone from pop stars to political propagandists learnt to bypass the mainstream and speak directly with their most ardent fans, there will no longer be any need to conjure up a statistically imaginary audience or stoop to the lowest common denominator. A company making fabrics for quilt-making might once have puffed itself up with advertising intended for its presumed patrons – a woman of a certain age, for example, who earned a certain amount or who lived in a particular kind of family unit. It might even have begun to find fabrics to fit the demographic. It probably worked well enough, but only at the expense of stereotyping its customers. As a weapon it was also unreliable, missing as many potential quilt-makers as it managed to pick off. Somewhere out there online, however, there is very likely to be the quilt-making equivalent of Moleskinerie.com, a core of enthusiasts who do not just have a passing interest in quilting but who live and breathe it. Talking to people like this and listening to them talk among themselves is likely to prove much more rewarding than guessing who might want to be your customer. It is also going to favour those with something distinctive to offer in the first place. Instead of having to dilute what is most original about their work, or cut it up for a hypothetical audience, they can lure in a flock of passionate fans to savour it, support it and spread the word.

*

When everyone from farm-lovers to notebook enthusiasts gets their own flock to fly with, it is as if we have all become teenagers again. If this is what is opening up beyond the mainstream, there is much to be hopeful for. Surrounding oneself with a fervent group of fans is proving one of the most reliable ways to grow original work. Inspire them enough and they will take it away and spread it around.

Faced with a boundless online ecosystem it is understandable that we are migrating to be with those who share our passions, whether they are far away or around the corner. But maybe we have lost something too in the collapse of the middle ground. During his research for FarmersOnly.com, Jerry Merrill told me he was struck by the fact that real-life farmers did not usually marry other farmers, but those around them in the local community. 'The farmer would marry the schoolteacher, presumably, or the person who ran the food store. They weren't necessarily marrying other farmers, but people who were farm-friendly.' Neither, one suspects, would they have felt much need to define themselves as farmers or farm-friendly. The rush to identify with others can blind us to what we have in common with everyone else. Jerry Merrill admits that his efforts to find someone for the divorced farmer who inspired his dating agency still haven't yielded a match. 'And to the best of my knowledge,' he says, 'she's still looking.'

7

Pigeon-holed

The problems with niche

On the dangers of ending up in little boxes

The butterflies hit you first, three and a half million of them, at the end of a vast Victorian entrance hall in West London in the largest cocoon ever built. The Darwin Centre is a bulbous, curved-concrete structure growing out of the side of the Natural History Museum. It is eight storeys high, surrounded by an enormous glass box, and within its walls lies one of the greatest collections of plant and animal specimens in the world. Walk along its fresh white corridors and many of them are on display – bees, ants, scorpions, grasshoppers and spiders. The cocoon was completed in autumn 2009, and its design is in keeping with its function: the building is sealed from the outside world, and its temperature and humidity are carefully regulated to keep out the tiny carpet beetles that would otherwise munch their way through the exhibits. But it also makes it the perfect home for its butterflies. Many of them are kept behind glass screens, their wings perfectly pressed and neatly pinned down, every shape and colour known to man, luminescent in their natural beauty.

The vast botanical and entomological collection held in the cocoon is a tribute to the diversity of life on earth. It is also testament to the work done by natural scientists to identify all these species and classify them into an orderly system. These are their trophies, after all, the products of four centuries of exploration and discovery by naturalists like Charles Darwin who travelled the world in search of new specimens. On their journey through its long corridors, visitors can stare through internal windows and see hundreds of real-life scientists at work, peering through their microscopes in open-plan laboratories. They are the only living exhibits; everything else is dead. Short pieces of video playing on screens scattered around the Centre show them out on field trips. Bugs are trapped, plants are snipped and butterflies are collected in huge nets. Each species is identified according to the traits it has in common; underlying it all is the science of taxonomy, which helps naturalists identify and sort what they find according to its place in evolutionary history. Once they have been properly classified and endowed with a Latin name, they're stuffed, pickled, glazed or dried and then laid in a drawer or mounted behind glass. The collection is changing all the time, as new species of insect and plant life are constantly being identified; it is estimated that as many as 90 per cent of the world's species are still awaiting discovery. The technology is changing, too. As the internet brings together people from all over the world around their interests, London's Natural History Museum, like many others, is taking steps to enlist the help of the public in its data collection. Thriving teams of amateur naturalists are bubbling up from the ether, each with its own distinctive area of specialism. There are online depositories dedicated to the latest sightings of squirrels, beetles and firefly, and Flickr groups where enthusiasts share observations of plants, trees or wildflowers. Some have posted evidence of entirely new species, and even helped to identify them. For the most part, scientists are excited at all this new activity. They do not have the time or resources to document everything that is going on in the natural world. The more eyes on the environment the better.

All this should be a little familiar. In the last few decades, as we slipped away from their grasp, the big beasts have employed pollsters and questionnaire sociologists to try to understand us better. To do so they have put us under the microscope, identifying ever more complex new species and sub-species according to the things we have in common. It didn't always work. Even as the traditional things that bound us together – social class, political affiliation and traditional religion – have fallen away in this new ecosystem, we still resist the identities chosen for us by the big beasts. At the same time, we are enthusiastically identifying with things online, replacing the traditional methods of bunching us together with our own home-grown classifications. There is a huge amount of diversity in our new ecosystem. By identifying ourselves according to the things we really like and flocking to be with those who feel the same way, it is easier than ever to find a place we can call home. But in our struggle to fit in, are we identifying ourselves too much with the things that we really like, trying too hard to wear the T-shirt for everything from Beanie Babies to *The Wire* to Barack Obama? Knowing your place in this new environment is great for those who have something distinctive to make or to sell, but it can force the rest of us into cocoons of our own making. The most glaring irony of our determination to define ourselves as different is that we can end up pigeon-holing ourselves in very precise little boxes.

2

The first box I ever ticked was White-Irish. It was on an equal-opportunities form in a job application, for a post managing a hostel for twenty-six homeless families in the London borough of Southwark. I got the job. While I am for ever grateful for the opportunity, and it led on to other jobs trying to house London's homeless, I can't quite shake the feeling that my ethnicity was one of the reasons I had been hired. I was only twenty years old, after all, with no experience of managing anything. There were good reasons why Southwark should want to collect information on my ethnic origins. The borough has always had a large and spirited Irish immigrant community, and earlier generations of them had been discriminated against, so it made sense to keep an eye on how many were getting jobs or failing to get them. When authorities identify people by their ethnicity, however, they risk forcing them into stereotypes and colluding with others who would like to define them as a species apart.

Many of those living in that Southwark hostel had only recently arrived in the UK, among them a young Turkish immigrant who was on the run from a husband who had tried to kill her. I'd been informed by her caseworker that she did not speak a word of English, but after three months of watching my attempts to communicate via elaborate mime she burst out laughing and confided that her English was almost perfect. The competition for permanent council housing was intense, and she was simply trying to do everything possible to secure a home for herself and her son. She just wanted to tick all the boxes.

Another immigrant who is suspicious of Britain's box-ticking authorities is the economist Amartya Sen. When I visited him in Cambridge he invited me for lunch in the magnificent dining hall of Trinity College, where for many centuries academics have presided over hundreds of undergraduates as they eat their lunch. Sen seemed very much at home, and so he should: in 1998, the year he won the Nobel prize for his work on economics, he was elected Master of Trinity, becoming the first Indian to head an Oxbridge college. Nowadays he divides his time between America, India, Italy and the UK; he remains an Indian citizen, but Britain is his spiritual home. 'Everyone has lots of identities, depending on the context,' he says. 'I like teaching in Harvard and I have an identity as an American academic. But I also have a strong identity as an economist, as left-of-centre, as an egalitarian.'

Sen's many-layered identity is one reason why he gets so annoyed when governments usher their citizens into different pens according to their religious faith, a form of classification often deemed to trump all the others. What begins by giving people room to express themselves, he says, may force them into an identity chosen by the authorities. 'That is what is happening now, here,' he tells me, a little indignantly. 'I think there is a real tyranny there. It doesn't look like tyranny – it looks like giving freedom and tolerance – but it ends up being a denial of individual freedom. The individual belongs to many different groups and it is up to him or her to decide which of those groups he or she would like to give priority. To classify Bangladeshis, for example, only as Muslims and overlook their

Bangladeshi identity is seriously misleading. To drown all that into a vision of "you are just a Muslim – please be moderate and likeable and replace all those extremist imams with moderate and likeable ones", that is simply wrong-headed.'

Sen has good reason to fear religious sectarianism. Seared into his political consciousness is the memory of how India suddenly fragmented in the period before partition, when people began increasingly to define themselves as Hindus, Muslims and Sikhs. 'This is the way that the British tried to interpret community divisions in India between Muslims, Hindus, Sikhs and Christians. To Indian nationalists, it looked a further example of divide and rule, emphasising the divisions. The way that the British are handling it today makes one wonder whether the cultural confusion that the British had then has now been brought back home.' He is surely right to point out that attempts at classification by the authorities are often clumsy and unwise. Religious and ethnic groups are often as internally divided as the rest of us. To what extent does it make sense to classify people as Muslim, for example, given the differences which exist between Sunni and Shi'a worshippers? How far can we bunch Sri Lankans together in a homogeneous group given the tensions between Tamils and Sinhalese? Worse, identifying people according to only one of their attributes can tell data collectors only what they want to hear. While it is true that black teenagers are disproportionately represented in street crime, careful analysis of the crime statistics by the British criminologists Marian Fitzgerald and Chris Hale showed that the category of blackness dissolves on closer inspection. Street crime, they discovered, is simply more prevalent in edgy urban areas where poverty co-exists with affluence, precisely the places in which young black men are more likely to live.

In any case, there is nothing primeval about ethnic or religious identification: affiliations can change rapidly along with the political temperature and are often stoked by those who want to take advantage of them. When the allocation of resources is tied to membership of such groups and overseen by 'community leaders' it encourages people to define themselves accordingly, which only reinforces the differences between them. Just as species in an ecosystem can sometimes find themselves in competition over a niche and the resources that go with it, dividing citizens into different species invites them to jostle for public resources, with each one protecting its own patch.

To political scientists, these new ways of identifying us are known as cleavages. Just like marketers, one response of savvy politicians to their escaping audience has been to separate it into different species and target the groupings accordingly. They are not only interested in different races and religions, but age groups too. As people live longer there are more generations around, and each of them – from great-grandparent to newborn child – can be said to have its own stake in the welfare and pensions system. Nor has it escaped their attention that older generations are more likely to vote than the young. The German elections of September 2009, for example, were built almost exclusively around the interests of older voters as the major political parties lined up to court the grey vote. Politicians of all stripes vied with each to canvass in retirement homes and spas, and to appear in the pages of formerly obscure periodicals like *Caravan* magazine and *Pharmacy Review*. It is not only German politicians who are hunting out age-based cleavages of support. For many years now Theda Skocpol, one of America's most distinguished sociologists, has been following attempts by both major American parties to play the country's different generations off against each other come election time. When politicians pit the interests of the retired elderly against those of poor children in the social security system, she told me, or hype the drain on public resources that might be caused by the middle-aged, they are betraying the universal origins of social security legislation which, at least when it was conceived in the mid-thirties, was supported by voters of all ages. In any case, she believes, their attempts to separate the generations are overstated. Since adult daughters still spend a huge amount of time looking after their elderly mothers, and most adults are in close contact with their ageing parents, the fate of the different generations is closely intertwined, and most voters realise that what's good for one is good for the others. 'Politicians haven't been very successful at persuading young Americans that older ones are the enemy,' says Skocpol. 'Most ordinary people don't identify with attempts to divide them by age-group, it doesn't really match their experience. But that doesn't mean that it isn't being done.'

Like those analysts who were sceptical of Gap's plan to cordon off its customers in tightly defined age groups, Skocpol has put her finger on the biggest problem with using one of our attributes to sort us into different species. It is simply not how we see ourselves. Despite the best efforts of politicians, she notes, only around a third of older Americans report a strong identification with 'the elderly' as a category. Many of us are also baulking at the menu of racial and religious classifications offered to us by officialdom. When researchers from the Institute of Public Policy Research approached people with the ethnic and religious categories listed in the UK census of 2001, most felt them a laughably inadequate way of capturing who they were. In their subsequent report 'You Can't Put Me in a Box', they found that 'young Britons in particular seem not to care much for tick-box approaches to identity'.

Many of the young people they interviewed seemed actively to be rebelling against the classifications foisted upon them by the authorities in favour of more fluid and multi-faceted identities of their own choosing. While they agreed that some aspects of one's identity were given or inherited, 'it was very important to our participants that their identity was something in which they had a choice and that that choice was a free choice'. Many seem to be resisting religious classification too. Shortly before that UK census was collected in 2001, an email was passed around suggesting that if ten thousand Britons identified their religion as Jedi Knight, the followers of fictional faith espoused in the *Star Wars* films, the authorities would be forced to recognise it as a religion. That was not strictly true, but that did not stop 390,000 doing it anyway, making Jedi the fourth largest religion in the country. Something similar had happened in New Zealand the previous month, and sizeable Jedi populations also identified themselves in Australia and Canada. We can guess at their motives. 'Do it because you love *Star Wars*,' the email concluded. 'If not . . . then just do it to annoy people.'

3

If the Britons interviewed by the IPPR were feeling boxed in by the classifications offered to them by the authorities, it did not stop them drawing boxes of their own. The only problem with the official categories, they felt, was that they were 'so broad and impersonal as to preclude or hinder any sense of who they thought they were as a unique individual'. When invited to, they were more than happy to replace them with ones of their own. Asked by the researchers 'who they are', they were more likely to name their values or personal characteristics than any of their demographic attributes. 'Rather than "male, 32, Scottish", for example, people told us they were "warm, bright, funny"; less Census category, more personal ad.'

This enthusiasm is hardly surprising. On our profile pages on Facebook and MySpace we have become accustomed to answering questions about who we are. It's as if we have become our very own questionnaire sociologists, profiling ourselves according to our name, age, gender and relationship status before gleefully compiling lists of our interests and favourite things. Everything is constantly updated, and the news of any change is broadcast to everyone we know. Mostly we seem to be telling the truth – MySpace's Chris DeWolfe believes that 98 per cent of his American users identify where they live truthfully and report important changes, such as getting married or moving house, soon after they happen. We are happiest, however, going beyond the usual classifications to add pithy identifications of our own. Facebook started out asking its new users to choose from a drop-down menu of political outlooks, but soon discovered that they preferred a text box in which to do it themselves. It did the same when it added its religious views box in 2006. Two-thirds of Facebook users choose to write something in the box, but they are doing so in unusual ways: the list of different religious beliefs now runs to many thousands (Jedi comes in at number ten).

When Peter Bobkowski and some of his colleagues at the University of North Carolina investigated how teenagers and young adults express their religion on MySpace, they found that a significant portion avoided identifying themselves according to their professed religious beliefs in favour of their own, hazier spiritual aperçus. There are good reasons why many us are striving to be different. Young people, Bobkowski told me, often want to distance themselves from mainstream religion and come up with something more novel. 'That's why you see all these little one-line creeds popping up,' he says. In an immense online ecosystem it also pays to distinguish yourself from the crowd, to put yourself under the microscope and identify yourself as a unique species before launching yourself in. In her book *Cold Intimacies*, Eva Illouz, an Israeli sociologist who has studied online dating and the pressures that it brings, writes that filling in the initial dating questionnaire 'makes one take a deep turn inward, that is, it requires that one focus on one's self in order to capture and communicate its unique essence, in the form of tastes, opinions, fantasies, and emotional compatibility'. It is important to get it right, she says, because otherwise no one you want to find you will do so. And just as you need to mark yourself out as unique, often it is only by specifying exactly what you're after that you can narrow things down to a manageable list of potential mates. 'For example, if you are looking for a blond, thin, non-smoker, below the age of 35, with a college education, unavoidably, a vast number of people will correspond to that description.' Just as with online retailing, the effect is to drive up the value of anything that sounds distinctive and depreciate the value of anything which can be had anywhere else. 'Because the internet makes us see the whole market of possible choices available to us (crudely put: it enables price shopping) in the actual encounter, we will usually tend to undervalue, not overvalue, the person encountered.' Unless we put a premium on ourselves, in other words, we begin to look generic and our value plummets. The result has been to make us more hawkish about finding love, more narrowly focused on finding what we take to be our best romantic fit. The problem, says Illouz, is that the chemistry which develops between two people cannot be reduced to a list of attributes. 'That is why we often fall in love with people who are very far from our prior notions, or why, when in love, we are willing to disregard an element which does not match our expectations, precisely because we attend to the whole, rather than to its parts.'

This ability to seek out exactly what we want is great when it comes to finding good things to eat and people with similar interests. Problems arise when we let those shared interests congeal into a worldview and we begin to identify ourselves as a species apart. There is evidence that, even before the internet, we have been itching to spend more time with people just like ourselves. In 2004 a journalist from Austin, Texas called Bill Bishop joined forces with Robert G. Cushing, a retired professor of sociology at the local university, to investigate patterns of population geography in the United States. Americans have always tended to move around a lot more than Europeans in search of work, but what Bishop and Cushing discovered was quite different: over the previous thirty years they had quietly been migrating to be around people with similar tastes, beliefs and values as themselves. 'The flows were selective,' reported Bishop in his subsequent book, *The Big Sort*, 'and they varied by personal characteristics, not broad demographic descriptions.' The magnitude of what was happening, he argued, could be adduced from a single statistic: in the 1976 presidential election 26.8 per cent of the nation's voters lived in 'landslide counties' where either candidate won by more than 20 percentage points, but by 2004 that figure had risen to 48.3 per cent.

It was an arresting figure, but Bishop's argument was not really about counties or states but local neighbourhoods, churches and volunteer groups; Americans, he said, were congregating in 'pockets of like-minded citizens that have become so ideologically inbred that we don't know, can't understand, and can barely conceive of "those people" who live just a few miles away'. In a hostile environment in which the old social moorings were disappearing, it seems, Americans of all kinds have been gravitating towards places and people they feel comfortable around. The upshot is that politics itself is dissolving into different ways of life, manifested in everything from people's attitudes to abortion to which magazines they like to read.

Democrats like cats, for example, while Republicans are more likely to own dogs. In the wake of the 2004 election two number-crunchers did some research into child-rearing and politics, and found a direct correlation between those who favoured spanking their children and voting for President Bush, while another claimed that he 'could find no better way to predict the vote for Bush' than how people were creating families (those who shacked up before marriage were much more likely to vote for the Democratic candidate John Kerry). Bill Bishop tells of the housing developer in California who surveys likely residents according to how strongly they agree with statements such as 'we need to treat the planet as a living system' and 'I have been born again in Jesus Christ'. But liberals, too, have been turning inwards to live in enclaves of their own. In New York the House of Elder Artists is a community of artists and activists in Manhattan, while the House of Tiny Egos is a bohemian commune in Brooklyn. The number of these so-called 'intentional communities' has grown, according to an organisation called the Fellowship for Intentional Community, from 614 in 2005 to more than 1300 in 2009. Sometimes the locus is no more than a postcode. In *The Big Sort*, Bill Bishop described how, after the invasion of Iraq, his neighbours in Austin, a liberal outpost in the staunchly Republican state of Texas, joined forces to print anti-war T-shirts and bumper stickers. 'The agreed-upon slogan promoted both place and policy. It said simply, 78704 PEACE. In Austin, zip codes have political meaning.'

Upping sticks to live with people with whom we feel an affinity is only the most extreme manifestation of our nesting and flocking behaviour – and one which is not available to everyone. Bill Bishop's book was written in the years after the 2004 presidential election, and his concern at how local geography had come to define many Americans was influenced by the battle lines that had been drawn in that campaign. Whereas pollsters like Mark Penn had spent their time trying to identify new groups of swing voters like Soccer Mom in the late nineties, George W. Bush's campaign team focused on isolating small groups of Republicans and getting them out to vote. Using high-tech data-mining weaponry they were able to zoom in on ever-smaller groups of core Republican supporters in their local neighbourhoods, even if they were surrounded by Democrat strongholds. What Barack Obama's team brought to election campaigning three years later was something new. By inspiring groups of volunteers to get involved and then putting them in touch with each other via a website, they were able to bring together small pockets of Obama supporters from all over the country and reinforce their identification with the campaign. Linking all these enclaves via a modern communication system made local geography less of an issue.

It is not only the internet that is helping Americans rise above geography and seek out like-minded people. That 2008 presidential election saw the nightly newscasts on broadcast networks humbled by a newer breed of cable operators, many of which cultivate audiences by deliberately feeding them news that fits their existing worldview. Fox News leans heavily towards the Republican right and is staffed by hectoring, bombastic anchormen like Bill O'Reilly. Its audience seems to like it that way: in survey after survey Fox is named as the TV news outlet Americans trust most. In an effort to match Fox's success, MSNBC (which is owned by the mainstream network NBC) has transformed itself into Fox's left-leaning alter ego, hiring similarly irascible talk-show pundits in an effort to reel in the convinced liberal audience. CNN, which has stubbornly remained in the middle ground, has watched its ratings drop through the floor: in 2009 its primetime audience was lower than that of MSNBC, the first time CNN had been beaten by any other network than Fox over a calendar year. According to data gleaned from TiVo, for each Democrat who watches Fox News there are now eighteen Republicans, and for every Republican who watches MSNBC there are six Democrats. When I asked the media analyst Michael Wolff about MSNBC, he scoffed, 'At least Fox's initial impulse is a truer one. They really believe in the politics. MSNBC don't, and to that extent theirs is a much more cynical move. But they're as much at sea as anyone else. How else are you supposed to sustain a TV news organisation in difficult times?' With their audiences heading for the exit, the big media beasts have been going after them in any way they can. But rather than trying to separate the general public into target demographics, as the mainstream networks have been doing for years, Fox and MSNBC simply carved it up according to its values.

Cable news outfits like Fox and MSNBC still have fewer viewers than the nightly newscasts of the broadcast networks, but they are gaining ground almost every year and their influence is echoing around the world. Their audiences do not just have an interest in political news – they can't seem to get enough of it. What this reflects, says the political scientist Markus Prior, is a growing disparity between news junkies and everybody else, who might see it in passing but don't much care if they don't. In some ways, there is nothing wrong with that. Political news, as much as politics itself, is now only of niche interest, as the growth of newspapers like *Politico* demonstrates. Underneath all this, however, is a more profound schism at the heart of American life. With the help of cable television and the internet, new communities of interest – everyone from Obama fans to the Tea Party movement that grew up after his election – are popping up and, in different ways, defining themselves against the decaying middle ground.

When another American political scientist, Alan Abramovitz, took a closer look at recent election data he discovered that by far the best way of predicting people's involvement was not their demographic attributes – their age, education, income, gender or race – but their passionately held partisanship for one side or the other. It was the moderates left in the middle who were much more likely to be uninformed and apathetic. 'The American public,' he asserts in his book *The Disappearing Center*, 'appears to be increasingly divided into two groups: the politically engaged, who view politics in ideological terms, and the politically disengaged, who do not.' To social scientists this phenomenon is often known as polarisation and Cass Sunstein, a scholar who now works for the Obama administration, is one of its most articulate critics. 'When people talk to like-minded others,' he says in *Going to Extremes*, 'they tend to amplify their pre-existing views, and to do so in a way that reduces their internal diversity. We see this happen in politics; it happens in families, businesses, churches and synagogues, and student organisations as well.'

Enclaves of like-minded people on the internet, Sunstein points out, can become fertile breeding grounds for extremist movements like Islamic fundamentalism. Polarisation, however, may not be quite the right word. The kinds of fanaticism he is talking about are really just the unpalatable underside of the progression from novice to fandom encountered in the last chapter, in which a person's interest in something intensifies as they learn more about it from experienced members of a group. Barack Obama, Sunstein admits, benefitted from something very like this in the course of the 2008 presidential election. The efforts of Obama's team 'created extreme enthusiasm for his candidacy . . . Obama supporters, especially young people, worked hard on their own to take advantage of existing networks and create new ones that would turn curiosity and tentative support into intense enthusiasm and active involvement'. The energy of Obama fans did not come only from defining what they were doing against the moribund middle ground of American politics. By putting them in touch with each other Obama's team encouraged them to identify with each other and the campaign, which only spurred them to become even more involved.

The strategy worked a treat, but in retrospect it might have had drawbacks too. While the middle ground shrinks, passionate groups of believers are making the running on either side of it. Just as many of us are looking for news we can identify with, in a democracy like this it is easy for politics to become no more than a badge of affiliation, a way – every bit as much as a Moleskine diary or the latest HBO series – to flesh out our identity and mark ourselves out. It ends with us inhabiting different encampments, each reinforcing its own position instead of engaging with what the others have to say.

*

The day after I walked around the cocoon at the Natural History Museum I phoned its Keeper of Palaeontology, Norman McLeod. I had wanted to talk to a naturalist about the classification of species, but just before I said goodbye I asked him what he made of how we humans separate ourselves into groups. He thought for a moment and came up with the following observation: 'Humans are highly social animals, and we don't like to be solitary and on our own. The collapse of the old groups together with the internet and globalisation forces us to choose which groups we belong in. When we classify ourselves on the internet and so on we're doing two things – we're trying to identify ourselves as unique individuals, but we're also trying to find a larger context we can fit into.'

In this new environment the audience is changing its shape. There is something for everyone, but very little for everyone. For the most part we are better off. The fact that we all used to watch the same TV programmes and channels, for example, does not mean that was all that we wanted to watch. Most of the time it just led to bickering over the remote control. Mainstream culture once provided us with a common vocabulary, but that was before the big beasts that controlled it stretched themselves thin in search of the median voter or viewer, or struck out wildly in an attempt to pick off new audiences. We don't have to watch the same thing to have something in common with our family or our neighbours; being able to see what we want whenever we want might even free us up to get to know them better. Besides, the rich diversity more than makes up for what we have lost. Flying off to discover things we are really interested in has brought all kinds of exotic species together in pursuit of what they are after. It has also helped us escape the pigeon-holes prepared for us by the big beasts. Even when we do all watch the same thing, we are often simultaneously coming together in more manageable masses online. One in seven Americans who watched the Super Bowl and the opening ceremony of the Winter Olympics in February 2010 were using the internet at the same time. The talent competitions and reality TV shows left behind on primetime broadcast television – what commissioners call 'water-cooler TV' – are a sort of sport too. They are games in which we pick a side, often watching along with our online flock.

Seedlings are growing up all shapes and size in this new cultural landscape, but there are gaps too. Our impatience means that we often lack context, that we cannot see the wood for the trees. In flocking to find a better fit with our environment it is easy to let the places that we land define us, hardening our opinions into immovable points of view: those who tweet their thoughts to like-minded groups of followers, for example, can end up playing to the gallery rather than trying to reach a broader audience. Fitting in to a place like this can often feel like squeezing ourselves into what is already there. In an essay for the *Nation*, the book publisher Elisabeth Sifton fears the worst. 'The World Wide Web is an ocean with few buoys to mark navigable channels of meaning,' she writes. 'The habitat is unnatural for the true life of the mind, politics or art. In this dystopia, one can scarcely get attention paid to new books except those that fit in with the flora and fauna already found there. True, you can easily reach niche audiences and specialty communities for your oh-so-unique book, but what of the general culture? How is your book being read? And in what manner might you try – say, ten years from now – to write something new?'

It's a fair point. In an environment thick with different nesting places and passionate flocks of followers, how do you go about attracting an audience for new things? The answer, surely, is to grow a place of your own.

8

Cult-ivate

On how to grow a niche

The year 2007, in which Paul Pressler parted from Gap, was also the year that a fifty-six-year-old motorbike dealer called Tom Hicks finally found his feet. A short visit to his showroom, in a dowdy and nondescript Orange County shopping mall several hundred miles south of San Francisco, is enough to see how he did it. Southern California (So Cal) Motorcycles is draped in the deep-red bunting, clothing and accessories of a single Italian motorcycling brand, Ducati, which only has a toe-hold in the American market. There are no other bike brands, and no generic parts or accessories to be seen. The floor space is crammed with Ducatis, signed pictures of Ducati riders obscure the wallpaper, a huge television screen blares out back-to-back races in which Ducatis cross the finishing line first. Nailed to the walls are Ducati bags, Ducati umbrellas, even a Ducati bath-robe. To the new arrival it looks less like a showroom than a shrine.

There is, however, more to So Cal Motorcycles than meets the eye. Hicks opened it in 2000, the year in which the Gap began to unravel, with sixty-five thousand dollars from the sale of his house. He started out selling Triumph bikes, another European make with only a minor share of the American market. His business philosophy, however, was a little unusual. Hicks refused to stock any generic equipment or accessories, reckoning that people could go to the bigger malls or the internet if that was what they were after. When the stockists for Triumph came calling, however, he asked for everything they had. 'Here is my concept,' he told me when I paid a visit to his showroom. 'If you love Triumph you don't want to come into a store, fall over a couple of Harleys, a few T-shirts and a salesman who doesn't know his ass from a hole in the ground. An enthusiast, when he walks into my store and sees exactly everything he can imagine for something he's totally into, his jaw hits the floor and he never has to go anywhere again.' When he landed the contract for Ducati in 2003, then, Hicks knew what to do: he built a separate showroom next door to house the new bikes. In 2005 he added another brand, Victory, and began work on a third showroom. After a spate of burglaries early in 2008 Ducati offered to remodel his store and Hicks gave over his entire space to the Ducati-exclusive refit, moving out Triumph and Victory into their own stand-alone showrooms across the way. In other words, within the same shopping mall Tom Hicks has three completely separate showrooms for three different motorbike brands. He walked me around them one by one, and they could not have looked more different – where the Ducati was decked out in deepest red, the Triumph showroom was a sea of dark blue and the Victory clad mainly in black. The only thing they share is the service department, where factory-trained technicians work on all three brands. For lovers of Ducati, Triumph or Victory, however, it is as if the others do not even exist.

With his neatly parted hair and his evangelical stare, there is something of the excitable schoolboy about Tom Hicks. He knows what it is like to be an enthusiast; his love affair with motorcycling has already cost him four divorces and one bankruptcy. It began in 1976 when he started a motorbike servicing shop out of his garage. When the workload became too much he sold up and went to work for Honda as a technician. After that he moved on to Triumph, where his proudest moment was teaching Pamela Anderson to ride the Triumph Thunderbird for her 1996 film *Barb Wire*. For the last thirty years he has competed in bike races and sports rides, and has even set five endurance world records. Whenever he would go to the races, he would take the kids along. Each time one of his marriages failed he would throw himself straight back into work. His work is what he was good at: Hicks has always had the knack of homing in on the unusual and the exotic, and then raving about it until other people share his excitement. The bikes that he sells at So Cal, after all, are minority-interest affairs that sell only a small fraction of the big five: Harley-Davidson, Honda, Yamaha, Suzuki and Kawasaki.

Hicks's love of the unusual and the recherché goes far beyond motorcycling. In 1987, when he still worked for Honda, he opened the only darts store for miles around; he had his fourteen-year-old son open the shop after school until he could make it back from work in the evening and take over. One day he decided to add an annexe selling archery equipment, and within a month the bows and arrows were making more money than the darts. Encouraged, he built an entire indoor archery range from scratch onto his existing store and made money for a while before everything turned bad in a spiral of divorce and bankruptcy. Experience has made Hicks painfully aware that being a die-hard enthusiast and a businessman often don't mix. At So Cal, however, his approach seems to work. 'Don't talk like I got money,' he says, when I ask him how his business is faring. When he started out in 2000 he had only three employees. In his first year he sold fifty-three bikes, in his second year that more than doubled to 116, he broke the two hundred barrier in 2003, and was selling three hundred in 2006 and four hundred a year later. By the time I met him, in 2010, he was selling over five hundred bikes a year, employing twenty-eight people and running a $3 million business. He had been voted the number one Triumph dealer in the US for the previous three years; in 2007 he had held the top spot for both Ducati and Triumph. Nowadays, he told me, he keeps a key for each of the three bikes he sells in case he should get the urge to take one out on the road. His employees call him Heff, after Hugh Hefner.

Hicks has long since stopped advertising nationally, and even in the phone book, in favour of direct email and a website. *Tom's Tidbits*, a personally written email newsletter, goes out once a week. 'People,' he says, 'spend more time now looking at their computer than they do anything.' Just as important, he runs some local racing events and makes sure So Cal is well represented at other races in the area. His showrooms are home to the local chapters of the Triumph Club and the Ducati Club, and for thirty dollars he offers both groups of bikers membership of his own clubs; in return they get discounts on accessories such as T-shirts, which make higher margins than the bikes themselves. The two groups of riders, he says, are walking, talking billboards for the shop. They even help out as volunteers at his events. By sating the appetites of small, highly motivated groups of enthusiasts, Hicks's idea is that they might go out and spread the word about his bikes. The point is not just to preach to the converted but to reach out to the general motorcycle rider and tempt them into the flock. There is some evidence that this is already happening, even without the help of Tom Hicks. Though the high-end, niche bikes he champions are not about to overtake the big five any time soon, their share of the market has been growing steadily over the last decade. When I ask him why that is, Hicks doesn't miss a beat. Nowadays, he says, everyone wants to be different. Even mainstream brands like Harley-Davidson end up accessorised and customised by those who buy them. But even though bikers want to be different from the norm, they also want to be part of something special, and that is where So Cal comes in. 'Motorcycling is such an individual sport,' is how Hicks puts it, 'but in the end everyone needs somebody else to ride with.'

2

Why did Tom Hicks prosper and Paul Pressler fare so badly? The two were not very far from each other in California, were almost exactly the same age and, despite working in very different environments, both were doing their best to sell things in shopping malls. It is possible that the answer lay in their talents as businessmen, but it seems unlikely. After all, Pressler came to Gap with an impressive track record whereas Hicks set up So Cal with little but a bankruptcy under his belt. In large part it is because of the terrain they were walking on. Both men were going about their business when they came up against a monumental fracture of mainstream culture – the missing middle. Paul Pressler's response was to train his sights on Gap's millions of customers. His plan was to use his data mountain to slice them into different groups and go after them one at a time. Tom Hicks's approach was superficially similar. Like Pressler, he understood that even though people say that they want to be different from the mainstream, they also want to huddle together in groups. Unlike Pressler, however, he did not set about pigeon-holing his potential customers. To begin with, he didn't really have any customers. He simply opened a series of motorcycling showrooms based around his favourite bikes and raved about them until he found others who shared his enthusiasm. Whereas Paul Pressler floundered in the middle, Tom Hicks managed to fit himself into the gaps.

The missing middle does not only affect retailers, and it is bigger than any shopping mall. So why should we care about these two? The answer is that, as we move further into our new ecosystems, it is the Tom Hickses who are better placed to succeed than the Paul Presslers. Hicks was a true believer: he lived and breathed motorbikes, and proselytised about his favourites to anyone who would listen. But he also realised that his customers needed to be built into fanatics, and so he gathered around his showrooms evangelists who loudly identified with his bikes. What he fostered, in other words, was a cult following. Cultish behaviour is reminiscent of wacky religious sects, so it is worth considering how they operate. A cult self-consciously distinguishes itself from the mainstream and its followers bind themselves together via elaborate rules or rituals; by tightly defining their boundaries, they inspire fanatical devotion. We are instinctively suspicious of what goes on in them, but most are not as scary as they look. Christianity, after all, started life as a cult before it evolved into a mainstream religion. Recently, however, the evolution has been in the other direction. In Western societies the big beasts of mainstream religion used to have something close to a monopoly on our attention, but in the last few decades most have been losing ground to evangelical groups, non-denominational sects and mega-churches that offer their adherents a more unique and personal relationship with God. A 2008 survey by Pew's Forum on Religion and Public Life documented the continuing rise of evangelical Protestantism and the decline of mainstream Protestant churches in the United States: 26 per cent of Americans now consider themselves evangelicals, versus 18 per cent who identify themselves with mainstream Protestant denominations. In some Western countries more people are defining themselves as religious than ever before, but instead of signing up to mainstream religions they are picking and mixing their own religious beliefs and – when they find ingredients that they really like – bunching together to find out more. Mainstream religion, meanwhile, is left wilting in the middle – religion for people who don't really like religion.

It is not only mainstream religion which is on the wane. Many of the cathedrals of commerce and culture we grew up with are toppling around our feet, and being replaced by jealously guarded affinities and passionately held affiliations. When we think back to Woolworths or *Gone with the Wind* we do so with a kind of lurid, Technicolor nostalgia. We are fond of them, but we don't really identify with them. Often we miss them not so much for what they were but because they remind us of something: a time when everyone shopped in the same places and watched the same things. Mainstream, middlebrow culture once brought us together, but now it is mostly barren and empty. Much of it was really only an exercise in packaging things up to find a broad audience. What gave it its power, the critic Gilbert Seldes pointed out in his 1950 book *The Great Audience*, was 'the tensions it managed to balance, the competing forces it was able to hold in solution'. As the energy moves from the middle to margins the centre can no longer hold. There will always be room for a few blockbusters, of course, throwing up fireworks in an effort to bring us all together. What is dying is the massive pile of stuff in the middle that no one is mad about – the films and television we watched because there was nothing else on, the newspapers we read only because we had time to kill, the high-street stores we wandered into because there was nowhere else to go. The middle ground is sinking beneath our feet. At some point in the last few decades it became, well, middling.

3

As the middle gives way, interesting new things are growing up all around it. One of them is the curious little coffee bar, within walking distance of my home on the Old Kent Road, where I wrote much of this book. When I first moved there it wasn't a coffee bar at all but a repair shop for motor-scooters and a home for its owner, a bluff New Zealander called Craig. To get inside Scooterworks you had to fight your way past broken-down Vespas and the posters, catalogues and ephemera that go along with them. Since Craig and his girlfriend Nathalie are catlovers, it is usually strewn with well-groomed cats. Craig also happens to be a coffee buff, which is why the walls are lined with old-fashioned espresso machines and coffee grinders. He and Nathalie decided to open a coffee bar. As the scooters gradually gave way to the coffee machine, tables and chairs grew to take up the whole shop and the workshop was moved off to a new location: Scooterworks had morphed into Scootercaffé. The following year they built a staircase into the basement and threw open an impromptu cinema; for their first season they joined forces with a local film society to show films that feature Vespas. To make the most of the Italian connection Scootercaffé took to selling sugary Italian soft drinks that would be difficult to find anywhere else. It has also acquired a reputation for the quality of its hot chocolate, pitch-black and as thick as lava. There is a Starbucks around the corner, but for anyone who cares about coffee, cats or scooters there is little reason to go there: this is a more convivial environment and the coffee is superb. In the evening it becomes a bar, and cats and motor-scooters are joined by bottles of wine and party-goers. The place is thriving.

Step outside Scootercaffé and you are at one end of a little stretch of high street called Lower Marsh, just by Waterloo Station. It is so called because it was built on marshland; this was once a sandbank of the River Thames. For almost two hundred years Lower Marsh has been home to a ceaseless procession of traders, stall-holders and retailers. The range of shop-fronts and architectural styles tell their own story; some of the stores here are over a century old and many of their owners have long memories. In common with most high-street retailers, they are feeling the pinch. The market stalls that were once a feature of the local area have all but disappeared along with the office-workers who used to frequent them. But there are signs of new life. In 2008, the same year that Scootercaffé was born, a gourmet grocer opened its doors on the other side of the street. Greensmiths is really an umbrella under which huddle five local independent retailers – a butcher, a fruit and vegetable counter, a wine merchant, a bakery and a whole bean coffee seller. All make great play of the naturalness of their ingredients and their provenance. The butcher, for example, calls itself The Ginger Pig and specialises in traditional breeds, 'preferring the superior flavour and fat content of the Tamworth Pig, with its distinctive ginger hair'.

Sales of this kind of speciality or gourmet food are growing faster than the rest of the food industry. In the United States, for example, they leapt from $26 billion in 1992 to $63 billion in 2009. According to the industry association responsible for them, they will account for a fifth of all food sales by the year 2015. But it is not only the distinctiveness of the produce that is turning so many of us into foodies. Just as specialty coffee roasters made good coffee into an experience that its drinkers could savour together, many gourmet retailers have transformed the appreciation of their product into a social occasion. Greensmiths, for example, hosts popular evening events – cheese tastings, wine tastings, even sausage-making classes. So does the knitting shop a few doors down. I Knit London opened in the same year as both Scootercaffé and Greensmiths, and labels itself 'a shop, club and a sanctuary for knitters'. Piled high on its shelves is a more extensive range than would be available in a department store, including the finer, hand-dyed yarns that would be difficult to find anywhere. But that is only one reason why people come through the doors. 'Knitters are obsessive,' one of its owners confides when I walk in. 'They want to knit as much as possible, so many of them need a constant supply of yarn. Plus they want to show off, as well as learn from others.' Stroll past on a Wednesday or Thursday evening and the shop will be colonised by knitters: you'll see them knitting, drinking pear cider and showing off what they have made. Many are commuters who like to stock up or do a little knitting before getting the train back home. Scootercaffé, too, has attracted a loyal core of regulars from throughout London and beyond. It surely helps that all these bohemian boutiques are gathered together in the same street, but what is striking is how little overlap there is between the different flocks of foodies, coffee-lovers and knitting enthusiasts. Like Tom Hicks's different showrooms, they are more like house churches than cathedrals of commerce, each with its own cult following.

Local enthusiasts like this are hardly enough to deal the big beasts a mortal blow. Even the bikers who congregate in Tom Hicks's showrooms all come from a 250-mile catchment area. But what if they could seek each other out on the internet? What is truly novel about our new ecosystem is that it allows ordinary people at the lower end of the food chain to gather from widely dispersed areas around the things they really enjoy. When we are able to flock around our shared interests we will no longer need someone like Paul Pressler to slice us up into groups, or even a Tom Hicks to put us in touch with each other.

Take those young fashionistas that Pressler's executives began to zero in on in the years of the century. Many of them, it turns out, quickly tired of being targeted by the big beasts and turned to streetwear instead. Streetwear is a fashion subculture that has grown up in the last decade as a spontaneous reaction against the efforts of brands like Gap and Abercrombie & Fitch to force-feed young people their own carefully researched ideas of what's hip. For the most part it has been fuelled by fans communicating with each other online about obscure collectible footwear, hoodies and baseball caps. Much of the conversation takes place across borders and is huddled around a new generation of 'product-oriented' magazines that evangelise about obscure products and their backstories. Hypebeast, for example, grew out of a blog first written by a sneaker fanatic in Hong Kong. It has since become a haven for sneaker fanatics all over the world; having twenty writers track the latest product releases and store openings of their favourite stuff has made Hypebeast one of the most popular fashion destinations on the web. Then there is *Antenna*, a quarterly New York-based publication that looks more like a book of arty photos than a fashion magazine. *Antenna* dwells on visual lists of all kinds of ephemera, and not just the fashionable stuff. One of its photoshoots consisted solely of a random selection of toothbrushes; another featured different kinds of chewing gum from around the world. Beside each photo is a name and a price – no other details are mentioned. The point, says its founding editor Tony Gervino, was to fight back against the cool-hunters and strip away the aura with which brands like to surround their products, 'telling people how they should wear things and what they should be interested in'. On one of his early editions, he told me, he even slapped a tractor on the cover. Even so, within a year of its launch in 2007 *Antenna* had 125,000 subscribers. One of its first advertisers was Gap.

We are only at the beginning of all this, but there are good reasons to be hopeful. Emboldened by online communication, a restless array of entrepreneurs, innovators and idealists is turning a trickle of people like Tom Hicks into a flourishing ecosystem teeming with exotic subcultures. Vibrant new nesting places are flowering all around us, cultivating passionate attachments in everything from rodeo to rap to revolution. Audiences are flocking from around the world – or around the corner – to find them. When markets become more global it is possible to grow a profitable niche around almost anything.

Take Apple, for example: with its traditional injunction to 'think different' and a fanatical following millions strong, the computer company is the world's most famous manufacturer of cult, high-end products. One of Apple's most iconic products is the iPhone, but by 2010 it controlled just 3 per cent of the world's market for mobile handsets. No matter: it shifted twenty-five million iPhones in the previous year and swallowed the lion's share of profits for the entire cellphone industry. Everything is being remade afresh, and there is plenty left behind on the bones of the mainstream to be nibbled away.

This is fertile terrain for anyone doing anything new. For the last two decades, big beasts like Gap have been spending huge amounts of time and money puffing up their brands with free-floating attributes to fit the characteristics their researchers discovered in their audience. Most of these new arrivals don't give a damn about the attributes of their audience. Instead, they focus on what is distinctive about their product and then try to lure in an enthusiastic audience to match. By staking their place outside the mainstream they no longer have to prune their work to fit the schedules and containers devised by the big beasts. They can give good stuff the time and space it needs to grow. This explosion of diversity does not have to mean the rise of amateurism. If being professional means having an area of particular expertise, it might even lead to greater professionalism.

It was always a mistake to confuse professionalism with drawing a salary, authority with institutions, and there is even less of an excuse for it now. Many of the big beasts have squandered their authority by sinking to the lowest common denominator or trying too hard to flatter their audience. In the vast ocean of information, what we could do with, in fact, are places where we can go to find guides and specialists, people who know their stuff and who are passionate about spreading the word. Authoritative new voices are going to spring up and some of the big beasts will recover the ones that they have lost. Even if they do, however, they are going to have to play a more humble role in this new environment. Stuck with expensive costs and equipment built up in the old ways of doing things, many of them are not really cut out for it. They are struggling to keep up.

4

The big beasts can take care of themselves. The rest of us are going to have to find a niche. Here is my advice: before you reach for the questionnaire sociologists or the communications weaponry, narrow your focus to make sure you have something that people can't easily find anywhere else. The missing middle does not mean the end of big audiences. The mainstream, after all, was never entirely synonymous with size. Whether your audience is local or global, however, it does mean having something distinctive enough for them to identify with. That sounds obvious, but it is surprising how many forget about it in the race to rustle up a following. If you are not really *about* anything, people can tell. When you do have something to show or say, find a real audience (rather than a statistically imaginary one) that believes in it and invite them in to nourish it. At this stage, quality is more important than quantity so the numbers can be modest. To protect your niche, you're going to have to build your authority over it. Get to know everything there is to know about it and cultivate that kind of connoisseurship among your audience too. Many hawkish consumers are tired of flitting in and out of different places and are looking for something a little more satisfying. Train them how to think about it and whet their appetite. It helps if you can surround it with a distinctive environment, a universe rich in material that becomes central to experiencing and understanding the work – and which allows fans to go as deep as they want. *Star Wars* was much more than just a film: it was a galaxy of related books, products, computer games and action figures. This was not just a merchandising trick; it gave rise to a richer backstory in which fans could immerse themselves. Telling a convincing story is a vital part of cultivating a niche because it helps to explain why all this stuff is gathered in one place. Otherwise you risk having your niche eaten away at and your stuff swallowed up. Anything that can be fully satisfied by easily digestible chunks, after all, makes easy prey for smaller predators.

With an enthusiastic audience in tow you can use them to help spread the word. You can also work harder to meet their individual needs. Often what is really valuable is not the thing you are making but the accessories, the paraphernalia and insider information essential for anyone who wants to be part of the flock. Form a club with privileged access to add-ons and use it to turn hawks into regular visitors, novices to fanatics. In the United States the religious publishing and products market was worth six billion pounds in 2008. Evangelical Christians know how to sell things like music, videos, products and accessories around the product – God. They also know that the best flocks are manageable enough for members to identify with, and to get to know other members. Since it is easy for almost anyone to find their biggest or smartest fans online, it is also much more practical to use them as a sounding board, giving them sneak previews of new work and asking their opinion. Often what works best is to get people together in a live audience. Audiences can be transformed simply by sharing the same space and talking to one another. As the energy moves from the middle to the margins we might well be on the cusp of a new golden age of live talk and performance, one with the intimacy of cabaret rather than the charge of the arena. If the film industry is going to survive well into the twenty-first century, Francis Ford Coppola has suggested, its screenings are going to have to get more imaginative and more distinctive. Directors might begin to attend live performances of their work, for example, 'like the conductor of an opera. Every night it can be a little different.'

In the eighteenth century thinkers used to believe that no species ever died out and that nature kept itself in a state of perpetual balance. 'Such is the economy of nature,' wrote Thomas Jefferson, 'that no instance can be produced, of her having permitted any one race of her animals to become extinct; of her having formed any link in her great work so weak as to be broken.' Now we know better. Nature is a chaotic and hostile place. Some ecosystems grow and prosper while others die out; species themselves are plagued by periodic bouts of mass extinction. When the ground cracked up beneath their feet many of the big beasts lost their nerve and headed straight for the middle ground in search of safety. Others who had previously commanded a clear and identifiable niche were tempted to do the same. It worked for a while but it left them without a place they could call home. What they should have done was to build a nesting place or refresh one if it had been eroded or eaten away, and use it to fit themselves back into their environment. Everyone wants to be unique, but what really distinguishes us humans is that we are the only species whose habits are being endlessly reinvented, who are really capable of digging our way out of trouble. Like Tom Hicks, all we have to do is shift our niche.

Select Sources and Recommendations for Further Reading

Introduction: The Missing Middle and the Gap

Darwin, Charles (ed. David Quammen), *On the Origin of Species: The Illustrated Edition* (New York: Sterling, 2008)

Golley, Frank B., *A History of the Ecosystem Concept in Ecology: More than the Sum of the Parts* (New Haven: Yale University Press, 1996)

Chapter 1: Out of the Whale

Biskind, Peter, *Easy Riders, Raging Bulls: How the Sex, Drugs and Rock'n'Roll Generation Saved Hollywood* (London: Bloomsbury, 1998)

Feather, John, *A History of British Publishing* (London: Routledge, 2006, second edition)

Greenberg, Clement, 'Avant-Garde and Kitsch', *Partisan Review*, 6:5, 1939, 34–49

Hotelling, Harold, 'Stability in Competition', *Economic Journal*, vol. 39, no. 153, March 1929, 41–57

Lambert, Gavin, *GWTW: The Making of Gone with the Wind* (New York: Little, Brown, 1973)

Myrick, Susan (intro. Richard Harwell), *White Columns in Hollywood: Reports from the Gone with the Wind Sets* (Macon: Mercer University Press, 1994)

Pendergrast, Mark, Uncommon Grounds: The History of Coffee and How it Transformed Our World (New York: Basic Books, 2000)

Radway, Janice A., *A Feeling for Books: The Book-of-the-Month Club, Literary Taste, and Middle-Class Desire* (Chapel Hill: University of North Carolina Press, 1997)

Rubin, Joan Shelley, *The Making of Middlebrow Culture* (Chapel Hill: University of North Carolina Press, 1992)

Shone, Tom, *Blockbuster: How the Jaws and Jedi Generation Turned Hollywood into a Boom-Town* (London: Simon & Schuster, 2004)

Silverstein, Michael J. (with John Butman), *Treasure Hunt: Inside the Mind of the New Consumer* (New York: Portfolio, 2006)

Thomson, David, *Showman: The Life of David O. Selznick* (New York: Knopf, 1992)

———, *The Whole Equation: A History of Hollywood* (New York: Knopf, 2004)

Whiteley, Paul, Patrick Seyd and Jeremy Richardson, *True Blues: The Politics of Conservative Party Membership* (Oxford: Oxford University Press, 1994)

Widdemer, Margaret, 'Message and Middlebrow', *Saturday Review of Literature*, 18 February 1933

Winkler, John K., *Five and Ten: The Fabulous Life of F. W. Woolworth* (New York: Bantam Books, 1957)

Chapter 2: Target Practice

Goldthorpe, John and Tak Wing Chan, 'Social Stratification and Cultural Consumption: Music in England', *European Sociological Review*, 23(1), 2007, 1–19

Penn, Mark J. (with E. Kinney Zalesne), *Microtrends: The Small Forces Behind Today's Big Changes* (London: Allen Lane, 2007)

Sosnick, Douglas B., Matthew J. Dowd and Ron Fournier, *Applebee's America: How Successful Political, Business, and Religious Leaders Connect with the New American Community* (New York: Simon & Schuster, 2007)

Weiss, Michael J., *The Clustering of America* (New York: HarperCollins, 1988)

Chapter 3: The Mole

Biskind, Peter, *Down and Dirty Pictures: Miramax, Sundance, and the Rise of Independent Film* (London: Bloomsbury, 2004)

Carey, John, *The Intellectuals and the Masses: Pride and Prejudice among the Literary Intelligentsia, 1800–1939* (London: Faber, 1992)

Clark, T. J., *Farewell to an Idea: Episodes from a History of Modernism* (London: Yale University Press, 1999)

Greenberg, Clement, 'Avant-Garde and Kitsch', *Partisan Review*, 6:5, 1939, 34–49

Hall, Stuart, and Tony Jefferson (ed.), *Resistance Through Rituals: Youth Subcultures in Post War Britain* (London: Hutchinson, 1976)

Hebdige, Dirk, *Subculture: The Meaning of Style* (London: Methuen, 1979)

Hobsbawm, Eric, *Behind the Times: The Decline and Fall of the Twentieth-Century Avant-Gardes* (London: Thames & Hudson, 1999)

Macdonald, Dwight, 'MassCult and MidCult', in *Against the American Grain* (New York: Random House, 1963)

Seabrook, John, Nobrow: *The Culture of Marketing, The Marketing of Culture*

(New York: Knopf, 2000)

Thomas, Frank, *The Conquest of Cool: Business Culture, Counterculture, and the Rise of Hip Consumerism* (Chicago: Chicago University Press, 1997)

Chapter 4: The Hawk

Baye, Michael R., John Morgan and Patrick Scholten, 'The Value of Information in an Online Consumer Electronics Market', *Journal of Public Policy and Marketing*, 22(1), Spring 2003, 17–25

Cocks, H. G., Classified: *The Secret History of the Personal Column* (London: Random House, 2009)

Davies, Nick, *Flat Earth News: An Award-Winning Reporter Exposes Falsehood, Distortion and Propaganda in the Global Media* (London: Chatto & Windus, 2008)

Downie, Jr., Leonard, and Michael Schudson, 'The Reconstruction of American Journalism', *Columbia Journalism Review*, 19 October 2009

Halavais, Alexander, *Search Engine Society* (Cambridge: Polity, 2009)

Surowiecki, James, 'Soft in the Middle', *New Yorker*, 29 March 2010

Twitchell, James B., *AdCult USA: The Triumph of Advertising in American Culture* (New York: Columbia University Press, 1996)

Williams, Francis, *Dangerous Estate: The Anatomy of Newspapers* (London: Longmans, Green, 1957)

Chapter 5: The New Nesting Places

Anderson, Chris, *The Long Tail: How Endless Choice Is Creating Unlimited Demand* (London: Business Books, 2006)

Edgerton, Gary R., and Jeffrey P. Jones (ed.), *The Essential HBO Reader* (Lexington: University Press of Kentucky, 2008)

Johnston, Steven, 'Snacklash: In Praise of the Full Meal', *Wired*, 15.03, March 2007

Leverette, Marc, Brian L. Ott and Cara Louise Buckley (ed.), *It's Not TV: Watching HBO in the Post-Television Era* (New York: Routledge, 2008)

Chapter 6: Birds of a Feather

Ariely, Dan, *Predictably Irrational: The Hidden Forces That Shape Our Decisions* (London: HarperCollins, 2009, revised edition)

Baker, Stephen, *The Numerati: How They'll Get My Number and Yours* (London: Jonathan Cape, 2008)

Becker, Howard S., 'Becoming a Marihuana User', *American Journal of Sociology*, vol. 59, no. 3, November 1953, 235–42

Benzecry, Claudio E., 'Becoming a Fan: On the Seductions of Opera', *Qualitative Sociology*, 32, February 2009, 131–51

Chatwin, Bruce, *The Songlines* (London: Cape, 1987)

Cohen, Adam, *The Perfect Store: Inside eBay* (New York: Little, Brown, 2002)

Heilemann, John, and Mark Halperin, *Race of a Lifetime: How Obama Won the*

White House (London: Viking, 2010)

Plouffe, David, *The Audacity to Win: The Inside Story and Lessons of Barack Obama's Historic Victory* (New York: Viking, 2009)

Chapter 7: Pigeon-holed?

Abramowitz, Alan I., *The Disappearing Center: Engaged Citizens, Polarization, and American Democracy* (New Haven: Yale University Press, 2010)

Bishop, Bill (with Robert G. Cushing), *The Big Sort: Why the Clustering of Like-Minded America Is Tearing Us Apart* (New York: Houghton Mifflin, 2008)

Campbell, Peter, 'At the Natural History Museum', *London Review of Books*, vol. 31, no. 19, 8 October 2009

Fanshawe, Simon, and Dhananjayan Sriskandarajah, *You Can't Put Me in a Box: Super-Diversity and the End of Identity Politics in Britain* (London: IPPR, 2010)

Illouz, Eva, *Cold Intimacies: The Making of Emotional Capitalism* (Cambridge: Polity Press, 2007)

Malik, Kenan, *Strange Fruit: Why Both Sides Are Wrong in the Race Debate* (Oxford: Oneworld, 2008)

Sen, Amartya, *Identity and Violence: The Illusion of Destiny* (London: Allen Lane, 2006)

Sifton, Elisabeth, 'The Long Goodbye? The Book Business and Its Woes', *The Nation*, 8 June 2009

Skocpol, Theda, *The Missing Middle: Working Families and the Future of American Social Policy* (New York: W. W. Norton, 2000)

Sunstein, Cass R., *Going to Extremes: How Like Minds Unite and Divide* (Oxford: Oxford University Press, 2009)

Chapter 8: Cult-ivate

Jacobs, Jane, *The Death and Life of Great American Cities* (New York: Random House, 1961)

Kolbert, Elizabeth, 'The Sixth Extinction?', *New Yorker*, 25 May 2009

Kricher, John, *The Balance of Nature: Ecology's Enduring Myth* (Princeton: Princeton University Press, 2009)

Seldes, Gilbert, *The Great Audience* (New York: Viking, 1950)

Acknowledgements

I should start by thanking those who talked to me: Dan Ariely, Claudio Benzecry, Trevor Bish-Jones, Peter Bobkowski, Aaron Bragman, Nicholas Clee, Dean DeBiase, Stuart Elliott, Andrew Fisher, Adrian Foxman, Armand Frasco, Andy Garbutt, Peter Gelb, Thomas Gensemer, Bill Gorman, John Harris, Tom Hicks, Shabeer Hussain, Eva Illouz, Murat Kantarcioglu, Brian MacArthur, Peter Mair, Norman McLeod, Jerry Merrill, John Morgan, Maura Musciacco, Craig Newmark, Scott Pack, Jane Penner, S. Abraham Ravid, David Reiley, Claire Robertson, Alex Ross, Dan Scheinman, Maria Sebregondi, Paul Sexton, Michael Silverstein, Theda Skocpol, Jason Squires, Martin Talbot, David Thomson, Art Twain, Tim Urquhart, Hal Varian, Alan Ware and Michael Wolff. I'm grateful, too, for a grant from the K. Blundell Trust, administered by the Society of Authors, which paid for the travel costs associated with some of these interviews. Toby Mundy helped me think about how the general subject might make for a book. Louise Dennys, Michael Schellenberg and Michelle MacAleese were all very supportive of my writing, and graciously introduced me to Toronto and Canadian readers when I went there to publish my previous book *Cyburbia*. Once again, my agent Elizabeth Sheinkman deftly arranged for the book's publication. Tim Whiting at Little, Brown made for a fantastic editor and sounding board; generous with his time and ideas, he delicately steered the book in the right direction at every turn. Zoe Gullen did a wonderful job in refining my prose into something more readable, Victoria Pepe kept a tight rein on the book's production and Sophie McIvor was enthusiastic about publicising it even before I'd finished. Toby Manhire and Janine Gibson of the *Guardian* and Neil O'Sullivan of the *Financial Times* commissioned piece which planted the seeds of some of these ideas; the interview with Amartya Sen in Chapter 7 was originally published in the *Guardian*.

Conversations with Adam Curtis have, as usual, helped immeasurably in whetting my interest in these issues. Thanks are also due to Clare Collins, Stephen Foley, Alex Guiton, Emma Harkin, James Harkin senior, the late Tom Harkin, Kitty Hauser, Mark Johnston, Bridie Kelly, Jemima Lewis, Eleni Panagiotarea, Martha Pym, Simon Ransley, Dominic Rubin and Yasmin Whittaker-Khan. Without their encouragement and their distraction, writing would have been a much lonelier business.

Index